# Dakota

# Dakota

Bette Wolf Duncan

Copyright © 2011 by Bette Wolf Duncan.

Library of Congress Control Number: 2011900764
ISBN:   Hardcover    978-1-4568-5366-2
        Softcover    978-1-4568-5365-5
        Ebook        978-1-4568-5367-9

All rights reserved. No part of this book may be reproduced or transmitted in any form or by any means, electronic or mechanical, including photocopying, recording, or by any information storage and retrieval system, without permission in writing from the copyright owner.

This book was printed in the United States of America.

**To order additional copies of this book, contact:**
Xlibris Corporation
1-888-795-4274
www.Xlibris.com
Orders@Xlibris.com

# Contents

DEDICATION ...........................................................................9

PREFACE ................................................................................11

ACKNOWLEDGEMENTS ....................................................13

THE LOUISIANA PURCHASE ............................................15
    Sacrifice Cliff .....................................................................18
    Red River Rose ..................................................................21
    The Lewis and Clark Expedition .....................................24
    The Quest ..........................................................................28

DAKOTA TERRITORY .........................................................29
    Red River Valley Early Pioneers ......................................32
    First Year On The Prairie .................................................37
    Soddy Dug into a Hill ......................................................39
    The Gold Rush Widow ....................................................42
    The Last Of The 5000 ......................................................45

MONTANA TERRITORY .....................................................49
    Shaney Ridge .....................................................................52
    Empty Cradle Sad .............................................................55
    Rustlin' in the Bighorns ...................................................58
    Rustlers' Roost ..................................................................59
    Goin' For Broke ................................................................61
    It Cost Me Mary Lou .......................................................64

STATE OF MONTANA .........................................................66
    That Pretty Patch Of Green .............................................68
    Memories Of Alvin Wolf ..................................................70
    Men From Way Out West ................................................80

    She Talked With Horses ............................................................. 82
    Dust, Grasshoppers, and Drought! ........................................... 84
    Black Sunday ............................................................................ 86
    Depression Years in Montana .................................................... 88
    Makin' Do ................................................................................ 90
    Field of Dreams ........................................................................ 92
    Mountain Man ......................................................................... 94
    The Red Lodge Rodeo .............................................................. 99
    8 Seconds From Glory ............................................................ 102
    Cowboys Don't Cry ................................................................ 103
    Man Of The Mountains .......................................................... 105

THE END OF AN ERA ................................................................. 107
    Cattle Drivin' Cowboy ............................................................ 109
    The Rancher's New Computer ................................................ 110
    The Times, They Are A Changin' ........................................... 112
    The Water Wars ..................................................................... 114
    Muddy Water ......................................................................... 116
    The Chronic Farm/Ranch Crisis ............................................. 118
    Cattle Country Trilogy ........................................................... 120

TOMBSTONES ON THE PRAIRIE ............................................. 124
    The Broken Hearted House .................................................... 125

BIBLIOGRAPHY ........................................................................... 127

# Dedication

This book is dedicated to a kind and dear daughter, Robin Duncan Barber; and grandchildren, Tasha Watson, and Blake, Caleb, Ashley, Shayla and Sherisse Barber. In the words of a stanza written for my late husband on our 45th wedding anniversary:

. . . .

What counts is neither fame nor wealth,
nor job or some degree.
What counts is joy and health of those
who share your family tree.
So what's the measure of our lives?
I'd say we're worth a lot . . .
not because of what we did
or anything we've got . . . .
but because we had a daughter
who had six worthy kids;
and all of them enriched us
with the worthy lives they've lived.

# PREFACE

It was my intent, in writing *Dakota* to present a birds-eye view of the transition of a segment of the Louisiana Purchase into the states of Montana, North Dakota and Wyoming. That goal was accomplished through the use of historical data meshed with Western poetry, with each poem contributing a relevant insight. There are thirty-three poems in this book. But if my goal has succeeded, *Dakota* is more than a collection of Western verse: It is a raft with thirty-three supporting logs, that has skimmed o'er the river of Western history.

Bette Wolf Duncan

# ACKNOWLEDGEMENTS

I am indebted to my sister, Dolores McMullen, for her input in this book. For over thirty-five years prior to her death, she did genealogy research, and collected records, documents, family photos and written accounts of maternal and paternal ancestors. When she died, I acquired immigration papers, property transactions, articles in papers, homestead affidavits etc. You name it, she had it! Without all of her work, this book would never have materialized.

I would like to recognize and thank the following artists for allowing me to present copies of their work: Bob Coronato, *The Horse Wrangler Gather'd the Morning Mounts: One That Hadn't Lived the Life . . . Couldn't Paint a Picture . . . To Please the Eye of One That Had!*; and Jeri Dobrowski, *The Little House That Grew*. Likewise, I am indebted to Margo Metegrano of www.CowboyPoetry.com who presented paintings on the *Art Spur* project to challenge poets; and who invited submissions of family historical data. This spurring and invitation generated many of the poems and family histories appearing in this book.

# THE LOUISIANA PURCHASE

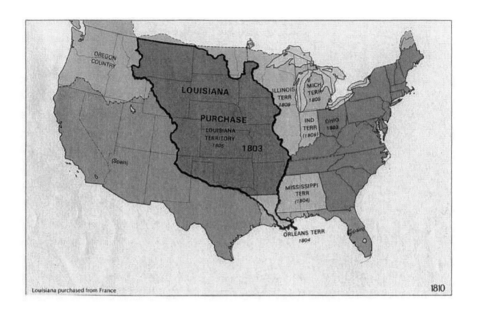

1810 map used courtesy of Library of Congress.

The Louisiana Territory, purchased for less than 5¢ an acre, was one of Thomas Jefferson's greatest contributions to his country. Louisiana doubled the size of the United States literally overnight, without a war or the loss of a single American life. It opened the way for the eventual expansion of the United States across the continent to the Pacific, and its consequent rise to the status of world power. The story of the way in which the United States acquired Louisiana reveals the foresight of Thomas Jefferson, who considered the purchase as one of his greatest achievements.

At the end of the French and Indian Wars in 1763, France lost all of its possessions in North America, including the French territory called Louisiana that extended from New Orleans up the Missouri River to modern-day Montana. Louisiana west of the Mississippi was ceded to

Spain, while the victorious British received the eastern portion of the huge colony.

When the United States won its independence from Great Britain in 1783, one of its major concerns was having a European power on its western boundary, and the need for unrestricted access to the Mississippi River. As American settlers pushed west, they found that the Appalachian Mountains provided a barrier to shipping goods eastward. The easiest way to ship produce was to build a flatboat and float down the Ohio and Mississippi Rivers to the port of New Orleans. From there goods could be put on ocean-going vessels. The problem with this route was that the Spanish owned both sides of the Mississippi below Natchez.

In 1795, the United States negotiated a treaty with Spain that provided for the right of navigation on the river and the right to deposit U.S. goods at the port of New Orleans. By 1802, U.S. farmers, businessmen, trappers, and lumbermen were bringing over $1 million worth of produce through New Orleans each year. Spanish officials were becoming concerned, as U.S. settlement moved closer to their territory. Spain was eager to divest itself of Louisiana, which was a drain on its financial resources. In 1800, Napoleon Bonaparte entered into a treaty with Spain, which returned Louisiana to French ownership in exchange for a Spanish kingdom in Italy.

Before the official transfer of Louisiana to French ownership had taken place, Spain revoked the right of deposit at New Orleans of all cargo from the United States. The closure of this vital port to the United States caused anger and consternation: commerce in the west was virtually blockaded. Meanwhile, Napoleon's plans in the Caribbean were frustrated by a rebellion of former slaves; and his colonial ambitions for a French empire were foiled in North America. Napoleon turned his attention once more to Europe. He decided that the sale of Louisiana would supply needed funds to wage war there. Napoleon and officials acting on behalf of President Jefferson closed a deal involving the purchase of the entire 828,000 square-mile Louisiana territory for approximately $15 million.

When news of the purchase reached the United States, President Jefferson was surprised. He had authorized the expenditure of $10 million for New Orleans, and, instead, received treaties committing the government to spend $15 million on a land package which would double the size of the United States. Jefferson's political opponents argued that the Louisiana Purchase was a worthless desert, and that the Constitution did not provide for the acquisition of new land. What really worried the opposition was that the new states which would inevitably be carved from the Louisiana Territory, would strengthen Western and Southern interests in Congress. They would also reduce the influence of Eastern interests in national affairs. President Jefferson, however, was an enthusiastic supporter of westward expansion. He held firm; and under his leadership the U.S. Senate ratified the Louisiana treaty in 1803. The rights to the Louisiana Purchase territory cost the United States $15 million, which came out to an average of less than 5¢ an acre.

Much of what is now Montana, Wyoming and North Dakota was acquired in the Louisiana Purchase; and the abundance of furs there was one of the keys that opened up the area. Indeed, the first white man in North Dakota (Verendrye in 1738) came on an exploratory visit to the Mandan Indians; and his trip was financed by a fur company. Lewis and Clark explored the area in 1804 and 1805, and one of their objective was to gather information on the abundance and distribution of fur-bearing animals. Later, many fur companies established forts and outposts to accommodate the needs of the trappers and to compete in the business of buying furs from the trappers and the various Indian tribes that lived there. Congress made temporary provisions for local civil government to continue as it had under French and Spanish rule; and it authorized the president to use military forces to maintain order. During the 1850s, west-bound settlers came into conflict with the local Indian tribes. To protect the settlers from Indian attacks, the army established a series of frontier forts.

One of the major Indian tribes in what is now southeastern Montana and North Dakota, was the Crow (also called the Absaroka or Apsáalooke). Some historians believe the early home of the Crow ancestral tribe was near the headwaters of the Mississippi River around Minnesota. Later the people moved to the Devils Lake region of North Dakota; and from there, they moved westward into Montana and Wyoming. The name of the tribe, Apsáalooke, was translated into French by interpreters as *gens du corbeaux*, people of the crow. Literally, it means "children of the large-beaked bird".

# Sacrifice Cliff

Northwest of Pryor, bordering the town of Billings, Montana, rises an arid, rock-ribbed expanse called the Rims. There was something inside the old weathered fortress that beckoned. You'd end up spending day after day hiking on its ledges and exploring its caves. If your eyes lacked the sight to hear the wild, racing hoofs pounding on the valley floor, they surely could hear a muscular, humpbacked buffalo or two snorting in the boulders here and there. And if you climbed to the top ledge and listened to the howling of the wind through the pile of rocks just east of the Devil's Kitchen cave, you believed the stories were true—that Indians haunted the Rims. Arrowheads were embedded in the earth. Indian carvings were on the rocks. And on the eastern edge of the Rims, there rose Sacrifice Cliff, every inch of which was inhabited by ghosts of warriors past.

The following poem is an account of an actual event that took place near Billings around 1854. Up to about the 1970s, the site of this event was deemed to be in northeast Billings, just north of the Midland Empire Fairgrounds; and located there, was a large marker that gave the history of this event. Since then it has been determined that the actual site is southeast of Billings; and the marker has been moved.

*The Lookout* by Charles M. Russell (1901)

## *Sacrifice Cliff*

It was the Moon Of Heat Waves
and all the creeks were dry.
Big black birds were gliding,
riding downdrafts, in the sky.
The warriors rode toward the cliff,
the children of the long-beaked bird-
in Indian tongue, the Apsaalookes;
Crow, the white man's word.

The Sun God soon, would ride off west,
packing up his golden light;
but they'd be dead before the dog-star
climbed into the dusky night.
Every breeze brought whiffs of pine
and pungent scents of gray-green sage.
None of it could ease their pain,
or stem their bitter rage.

Prairie dogs and sage hens
still scrambled wildly on the range;
but miles and piles of buffalo skulls
spoke loudly of the chilling change.
No medicine could conjure back
the herds of buffalo,
that always had provided food
and clothes and shelter for the Crow.

Their hunting days were over
and the life they knew was done.
The Crow would have to start anew.
A new day had begun.
The Crows could fight the soldiers
and the bullets they possessed,
but they couldn't fight the pox-fire
the white men brought out west.

Their village had been scourged by pox
and nearly half had died.
Montana had been washed by blood.
Grief had swept the country side.
Blood had seeped into the soil
where now the sagebrush grew;
and blood had stained the memory
of every lodge they knew.

There was blood upon the prairie,
and blood upon the sun.
Tears flowed deep inside them,
but their ride was almost done.
The One Who Had Made Everything
was angry with the Crow.
The tribe owed him a sacrifice
before He'd ease their woes.
The warriors gathered on the Rims
around a rocky bluff.
Perhaps the sacrifice they'd give
that day, would be enough.
With blindfolds on their ponies
down off the cliff they plunged,
their sacrifice completed
and their tribal debt expunged.

\* \* \*

The long-beaked birds were clustered
near the cliff on scraggly trees,
gliding, riding downdrafts,
cutting circles in the breeze.
It was The Moon Of Heat Waves.
The grass was brown and dried.
But the grass turned black
with long-beaked birds,
the day the warriors died.

# Red River Rose

*Drawing of a Red River Cart by C. W. Jeffries. From the newspaper, Minnesota Gazette, St. Paul, MN; July 22 1851.*

In 1818 the Red River Valley located in Southern Canada became a part of the United States by treaty with Great Britain. By 1820, Pembina (in what is now North Dakota, near the Canadian border) became an important hunting and trading center and a major link in the transportation network that developed between St. Paul and the "lower" Red River Basin. There were trails along both sides of the river to carry products to Canada or to St. Paul. The Red River Carts, pulled by oxen, were uniquely designed to make it easier and cheaper to supply the Red River settlements from Minnesota than from eastern Canada. The earliest trails led south from Pembina. By 1850, hundreds of carts were making the trip each year.

A typical cart weighed about four hundred pounds and could carry eight hundred pounds. The heart of the cart was a pair of heavy, parallel, twelve foot long shafts. The single draft animal stood between the shafts to pull. The box rested on the shafts, and was fastened to keep it in place. The corner posts and side rails of the box were ingeniously located to allow side boards to be slipped in to keep objects from falling out of the cart. The all wood carts were easy to repair with wood found along the route. The hubs were left ungreased because trail dust would mix with lubricants and work like sandpaper. So they squeaked. Nearly every account of Red River carts mentions the annoying squeal of the carts.

When a number of these heavily laden carts were in a train or company, they were conveyed across a stream or water on easily constructed rafts. When there were only a few carts and they were light, the wheels were taken off, laid on a buffalo hide or two, sewn together, and made water tight. The stiff hide was then drawn up and tied so as to form a canoe, with the wheels constituting the frame work of the bottom. This hide canoe would float 1000 to 1200 pounds. A canoe of this kind was constructed in a few minutes.

By the 1840's, regular trade had been established between the Red River and St. Paul. In an article appearing in the *Minnesota Democrat*, St. Paul, on July 22, 1851, it was estimated that about five hundred carts had arrived to trade hides and furs for necessities such as tobacco, salt and other groceries. The article further states that the people of the Red River, who were mostly half-breeds, relied on buffalo, in addition to furs, for their exports and prosperity. They held two summer hunts; and the participants consisted of around 600 men with their families. The women and older children were employed in cutting up and drying the meat. They took with them from 1,300 to 1,400 Red River ox carts, each of which would hold the product of from nine to ten buffalo. Their hunting plains were very extensive, extending to the Missouri River.

The Red River carts were sufficiently important in the annals of Minnesota to have an engraving of one placed on the postage stamp that commemorated a century of Minnesota history.

### *Red River Rose*

Rose! Rose! My Red River Rose!
You can keep your silk beauties.
The one that I chose
was a leather clad half-breed,
my Red River Rose.
Her Pa was a trapper,
her mother, a Sioux,
and she knew that Red River
like few trappers knew.

She was savvy and shrewd,
with a head full of smart.
She filled load after load
in her Red River cart.
Load after load
of Red River furs;
and the top grade of beaver
and otter were hers.

My Red River Rose
with her midnight-black braids
and spirit as tranquil
as cool summer glades.
There came a day
when Rose fancied me
and I was content
as this poor man could be.

You can keep your silk beauties
all clad in fine lace;
with bonnets a' framing
a soft, powdered face.
Me—I got Rose
with her head full of smart;
and a heart that's as big
as her Red River cart.

# The Lewis and Clark Expedition

In February, 1803, at the urging of then President Thomas Jefferson, Congress approved spending $2,500 for a small U.S. Army expedition. (The final cost was $38,727.) Their assignment was to ascend the Missouri River to its source, cross the continental divide, and follow the Columbia River to its mouth at the Pacific Ocean. Jefferson chose 28 year-old Meriwether Lewis as leader for the group he called the Corps of Discovery. Lewis selected a former army comrade, 32-year-old William Clark, to be his co-leader. The expedition began May 14, 1804, as the group left Camp Wood River (Illinois). The expedition returned to St. Louis on September 23, 1806.

There were 33 people, including 29 participants that started the expedition at Camp Wood River. They then followed the Missouri River westward. Eventually, the Lewis and Clark Expedition established relations with two dozen indigenous nations. (Without their help, the expedition would have starved to death or become hopelessly lost in the Rocky Mountains.) Accompanying them was a Canadian trapper, Touissant Charbonneau, and his native Indian wife, Sacajawea, along with their infant son, nicknamed "Pompei". She acted as an interpreter on their journey to the Pacific Ocean.

During the course of his travels through what is now the State of Montana, Clark etched his name on a rock near present day Pompey's Pillar, Montana. (This town was named after Sacajawea's infant son.) The etching, in script, reads as follows:

Wm Clark<br>July 25 1806

Though Jefferson stated in one letter that the goal was to find a "direct & practicable water communication across this continent, for the purposes of commerce" (the Northwest Passage), the expedition actually had several goals: to explore and map the Louisiana Purchase, and to establish trade with the native peoples along the Missouri River. Jefferson also wanted to establish a U.S. claim of "Discovery" to the Pacific Northwest and Oregon territory by documenting an American presence there before Europeans could claim the land. According to some historians, Jefferson understood he would have a better claim of ownership to the Pacific Northwest if the team gathered scientific data on animals and plants; so this also became an objective.

The U.S. mint prepared special silver medals with a portrait of George Washington and had a message of friendship and peace, called Indian Peace Medals or peace medals. The soldiers were to distribute them to the nations they met. They were expected to act as symbols of U.S. sovereignty over the indigenous inhabitants. The expedition also prepared advanced weapons to display their military firepower. They also carried flags, gift bundles, medicine and other items they would need for their journey. Much time went into ensuring a sufficient supply of these items.

The Lewis and Clark Expedition gained an understanding of the geography of the Northwest and produced the first accurate maps and description of the area. During the journey, Lewis and Clark drew about 140 maps. The expedition documented natural resources and plants that had been previously unknown to Euro-Americans, though not to the indigenous peoples. The expedition recorded more than 200 plants and animals that were new to science and noted at least seventy-two different Indian tribes. Their visit to the Pacific Northwest, maps, and proclamations of sovereignty with medals and flags were legal steps needed to claim title to the indigenous natives' lands under the Doctrine Of Discovery.

Under this doctrine, title to lands lay with the government whose subjects explored and occupied a territory whose inhabitants were not subjects of a European Christian monarch. The doctrine has been primarily used to support decisions invalidating or ignoring native aboriginal possession of land in favor of colonial or post-colonial governments. Jefferson had the expedition declare "sovereignty" and demonstrate their military strength to ensure native tribes would be subordinate to the US, as European colonizers did elsewhere. This was "an extension of American power", not simply a scientific journey, though it added a significant amount of knowledge to scholars.

Indian Peace medal, obverse (left) and reverse (right)

33 permanent crew members of the Corp of Discovery, accompanied Lewis and Clark on their expedition. In addition, there were two French-Canadian fur traders, one of whose Indian wife was the interpreter, Sacajawea. She took her 55-day old infant boy with her. Captain Clark affectionately nicknamed him "Pompei" and "Pompy" for his "little dancing boy" antics. The crew members were of white, black, and red racial origins, plus mixtures of the three. The oldest among the men was the French Canadian fur trapper, Touissant Charbonneau, who was 47 years old. Sacajawea was a teenager thought to be approximately 17.

All the men were hand-picked by the two officers for their survivor skills—their knowledge of the frontier and native tongues, along with their proficiency in hunting, woodcutting, and other specialized craftsmanship. Lewis, on January 15, 1807, in transmitting to the Secretary of War his roll of the men who accompanied him on his exploring mission "through the continent of North America," gave praise and gratitude collectively to the members of the Corps of Discovery:

*With respect to all those persons whose names are entered on this roll, I feel a peculiar pleasure in declaring, that the Ample support which they gave me under every difficulty; the manly firmness which they evinced on every necessary occasion; and the patience and fortitude with which they submitted to, and bore, the fatigues and painful sufferings incident to my late tour to the Pacific Ocean, entitles them to my warmest approbation and thanks; nor will I suppress the expression of a hope, that the recollection of services thus faithfully performed will meet a just reward in an ample remuneration on the party of our Government." —Meriwether Lewis, Captain 1st U.S. Regt. Infty.*

*Lewis and Clark on the Lower Columbia River* by Charles M. Russell

## The Quest

An endless stretch of God knows what!
Only Indians knew.
Before their enterprise was done,
they meant to know it too.

Lewis and Clark. Their names alone
conjure up the quest
that stretched across the continent
and opened up the West.

But Charlie Russell saw much more
than just those famous two.
He saw a Black and Indian,
and a valiant, steadfast crew.

In his painting, he depicts
clearer far than words,
the obstacles that they all faced;
the hardships all endured.

As much as any other man,
he knew the untamed West.
He painted in his pictures,
the rigors of their quest.

Besides those two, it took a crew,
an Indian and a Black,
to pierce the unknown wilderness
and then to bring them back.

Russell's painting tells us much
of what the painter knew:
it took a Black, an Indian,
and a brave and stalwart crew.

# DAKOTA TERRITORY

The Territory of Dakota became an organized territory on March 2, 1861. The Dakota Territory consisted of the northern most part of the land acquired in the Louisiana Purchase by the United States. The name refers to the Dakota branch of the Sioux tribes which occupied the area at the time. Most of the Dakota Territory was formerly part of the Minnesota and Nebraska territories. Upon creation, the Dakota Territory included much of present-day Montana and Wyoming. By 1868, creation of new territories reduced the Dakota Territory to the present boundaries of North and South Dakota. The territory as reduced, existed until 1889, when the final extent of the reduced territory was split and admitted to the Union as North and South Dakota.

The admission of two states, as opposed to one, was done for a number of reasons. The two population centers in the territory were in the northeast and southeast corners of the territory, several hundred miles away from each other. On a national level, there was pressure from the Republican Party to admit two states to add to their political power in the Senate. A century later, with the populations of the two states at low levels, there were discussions of reuniting them as "Dakota", but this has never been seriously considered. Montana was admitted as a state in 1889 along with North and South Dakota; and Wyoming gained statehood a year later, in 1890.

The territory's major cattle markets were Belle Fourche in what is now South Dakota, and Medora in what is now North Dakota. While not as famous today as Kansas cow towns such as Abilene and Dodge City, these Dakota Territory towns were particularly important to the livestock industry during the long drive era. Belle Fourche, fifteen miles north of Deadwood, became the world's largest primary cattle shipping center by 1890, pasturing from seven hundred to eight hundred thousand head by 1884. Medora, two hundred miles north and the site of North Dakota's round-ups, became a nationally known cow town because of two internationally known cattlemen who ranched there. They were the French aristocrat Marquis de Morés and Theodore Roosevelt. The 1886 round-up there and in eastern Montana was one of the largest in the history of the cattle industry.

While the Dakota Territory was open for settlement in 1863, few settlers came to North Dakota due primarily to Indian attacks. In 1862, Sioux Indians massacred hundreds of settlers in Minnesota. Some of these then fled to the Dakota Territory. By 1870, North Dakota only had a population of around 2,400 people. But that all changed with the Black Hills gold rush that began in about 1874 and reached a peak in 1877. Prior to the gold rush, the Black Hills were inhabited by Native Americans (primarily bands of Sioux). The United States government recognized the Black Hills as belonging to the Sioux by the Treaty of Laramie in 1868. Despite being within Indian territory, and therefore off-limits, white Americans were increasingly interested in the gold-mining potential of the Black Hills.

The large placer gold deposits of Deadwood Gulch were discovered in November 1875. In 1876, thousands of gold seekers flocked to the new town of Deadwood, although it was still Indian land. The Sioux sought to protect their rights, and resisted violently. Nevertheless, the gold seekers continued, unabated. The U.S. government could not keep settlers out. In fact, the Black Hills produced 10 percent of the world's gold supply over the next one 125 years.

By 1872, territorial officials considered harvesting the rich timber resources of the Black Hills, and floating them down the Cheyenne River to the Missouri, where new plains settlements needed lumber. Geographical studies suggested the prospect of rich mineral resources. When a commission approached the Red Cloud Agency about the possibility of the Lakota's signing away the Black Hills, Colonel John E. Smith noted that this was "the only portion [of their reservation] worth anything to them". And he concluded that "nothing short of their annihilation will get it from them".

The Great Sioux War of 1876-77 (also known as the Black Hills War) was a series of battles and negotiations between the Lakota and Northern Cheyenne, and the United States. Perhaps the most famous of these battles was fought at the Little Bighorn in what is now Montana. Lt. Col. George Armstrong Custer and the Seventh Cavalry were ordered out from the main Dakota column to scout the Rosebud and Bighorn River valleys. On June 25, 1876, they encountered a large village on the west bank of the Little Bighorn. The U.S. troops were seriously beaten in the Battle of the Little Bighorn and nearly 270 men were killed, including Custer.

The continuous military campaigns and the intensive diplomatic efforts finally began to yield results in the early spring of 1877 as large numbers of northern bands began to surrender. The war was finally ended with another treaty, in which the Lakota ceded a fifty-mile strip along the western border of their reservation, plus some additional lands. This gave the United States legal title to the Black Hills and legalized the gold hunters and camp followers in Custer City, Deadwood, and other boom towns in the Black Hills.

The Indians were forcibly confined to reservations. Later, in 1890, a Ghost Dance ritual on the Northern Lakota reservation at Wounded Knee, South Dakota, led to the army's attempt to subdue the Lakota. During this attempt, gunfire erupted, and soldiers killed up to three hundred Indians, mostly old men, women, and children. Long before this, the means of subsistence and the societies of the indigenous population of the Great Plains had been destroyed by the slaughter of the buffalo, driven almost to extinction in the 1880s by indiscriminate hunting.

The railroads were the engines of settlement in the territory and, later, the state. The Northern Pacific Railroad was given land grants by the federal government so that it could borrow money to build its system. The federal government kept every other section of land and gave it away to homesteaders. At first, the railroad sold much of its holdings at low prices to land speculators in order to realize quick cash profits, and also to eliminate sizable annual tax bills. By 1900, the company changed its land policies after realizing that it had been a costly mistake to have sold so much land at wholesale prices. With better railroad service and improved methods of farming the Northern Pacific easily sold what had been heretofore "worthless" land directly to farmers at good prices. It operated agencies in Europe that promoted its lands and brought families over at low cost.

# Red River Valley Early Pioneers

By the 1860s, the fur trade in the Red River Valley began to decline. In 1862, the Homestead Act was passed by the U.S. Congress, giving title to 160 acres of unoccupied public land to each homesteader on payment of a nominal fee and upon five years of residence on the claimed land. But it was not until a survey was completed that the public land in the Red River Valley was actually available for homesteading. The Red River of the North runs through one of the most fertile valleys in the United States; and as it flows north to Canada it forms the boundary between North Dakota and Minnesota. Near the river's headwaters on the bank of the Bois de Sioux is Wahpeton, North Dakota, the second white settlement in North Dakota. (Pembina, a fur-trading post near the Canadian border, was the first.)

Morgan T. Rich was the first settler in this area. My great-grandfather, Mathias (Matt) Lorenc (Lawrence) (1844-1910), immigrated to the United States in 1866, with his parents and his cousin Alva (Albert) Chezik. They were from a small village in the vicinity of what is now Prague, Czechoslovakia. In 1871, Great-grandfather Matt and his cousin, Albert, joined Rich in Wahpeton. Both occupied and asserted claims under "squatter's rights".

Within the year, they were joined by Matt's sister and brother-in-law, Mr. And Mrs. Lorene (Lawrence) Formaneck and other relatives of the Cheziks. Of the sixteen earliest settlers including M. T. Rich, eight of them are relatives from Bohemia. Currently in Wahpeton, there is a monument that commemorates the role played in the founding of the town by pioneer Catholics: Mathias Lawrence, Albert, Joseph and Frank Chezik, and Joseph and Frank Formanek. There is a second monument that commemorates the first Mass* conducted in the Albert Chezik dug-out.

These Bohemian immigrants were of peasant stock belonging to a class of small farmers that were still suffering from vestiges of serfdom. Joseph II (1780-1790) abolished serfdom; but in response to pressures from the nobility, his successor restored many feudal obligations. Serfdom was not completely abolished in Bohemia until 1848. My great-grandfather and his relatives remained *de facto* serfs for many years after the abolition of serfdom. A full account of the conditions in Bohemia that led to their exodus and the details of their settlement in Dakota Territory appear in

***Collections of the State Historical Society of North Dakota***, Vol. IV, O. G. Libby, Editor (1913). This collection includes photos of these relatives, including the following, among others:

*Top*, Mr. and Mrs. Albert Chezik
*Bottom*, Mr. and Mrs. Mathew Lorenc (Lawrence)

Additional accounts of these early Bohemian settlers, all of whom were relatives, is to be found in ***Early History of North Dakota*** by Colonel Clement A. Lounsberry, (1919). The author was founder of the *Bismark Tribune*. See also, ***Memories of Josephine Jurgen*** and ***Biography of Joseph Chezik*** by L. J. Connolly, Wahpeton, N.D. (1937).

My grandfather Frank Lawrence was the first baby boy born in Wahpeton. Below is a wedding photo of him and my maternal grandmother, Mary Holecek, along with attending relatives, Charles Frank Chezik and Elizabeth Holecek.

At page 72 of the State Historical Society account appears the following statements:

*They [the Bohemians] are hard workers, and have little faith in schemes to save work. They give the same amount of energy to the virgin soil of North Dakota as they did to the crowded, and much-used soil of old Bohemia.*
*The Bohemians are naturally fond of music. Hardly a home is without its musical instruments, and there are always one or more performers in each family. The violin is the favorite instrument . . . .*

Following is a copy of a treasured family photo. *Left to right:* Theodore Chezik, John Chezik, and Walt Zajie.

Wahpeton was the opening wedge for settlement on the west side of the Red River; and it was the southern gateway to the Red River Valley. It was through this area that many homesteaders passed on their way west. As the frontier pushed westward to the high plains, many new emigrants found themselves getting off a train into a sea of grass and little else. Early homesteaders burrowed into hillsides before wooden cabins were built. They found a durable building material beneath their feet. Buffalo grass was short and tough with a dense tangle of roots; it held its shape when cut. Living in sod houses, however, presented many obstacles. The soddy leaked continuously. Women reportedly held umbrellas over their stoves while cooking. Tarps were hung on the ceiling to catch particles of dirt that fell. Living creatures shared the sod dwellers' space as well. Snakes, mice, and bugs were everyday inhabitants of the sod house.

Things like doors and windows were very expensive items. Often, the doorways were covered by a blanket until wood could be bought or obtained to build a door. The windows were framed with wood. Actual glass was rare as it had to be shipped from the Eastern cities. People covered their windows with blankets or used greased, oiled paper for the covering. In

1872 (ten years after the passage of The Homestead Act and two years after Matt Lawrence and his relatives settled in Wahpeton), Montgomery Ward marketed windows and frames for $1.25, and the railroads carried these and other supplies to the Great Plains frontier. (A railroad was built in the Wahpeton area around 1874.) Eventually these homesteaders progressed from their primitive dug-out, hillside soddies to more hospitable cabins, wooden houses or more complex and comfortable sod homes. They did so as soon as they could afford it. They learned and were innovative. The early pioneers paved the way for the influx of homesteaders that followed them.

# First Year On The Prairie

Though blizzards whipped the soddy,
still it rang with vibrant sound.
There was music every Sunday
on its floor of frozen ground.
It was Sunday! It was Sunday!
Our solemn mood turned mellow,
when Matt and Al played violins
and Lawrence played the cello.

Though the Arctic wind was blasting
and their misery was profound,
folks gathered every Sunday
and the soddy would resound
with fiddles and with singing—
voices ringing with good cheer—
but intertwining always
with the undertones of fear.

There was fear about the winter.
They should have had more sense.
Their food supplies were meager;
and their suffering was intense.
Their first year on the prairie,
and they'd learned! They would survive!
They'd make it through this winter
and come out of it alive!

They'd learned! And come next winter
they'd chink their soddy tight.
They'd plank the floor; more staples store;
prepare for winter right.
Till then, they'd sing on Sunday,
every Sunday after Mass,
until they'd sing and dance again
upon the green, green grass.

Matt and Al played violins
and Lawrence played the cello;
and the rest would join in singing
till the solemn mood turned mellow.
There was music every Sunday
on the frozen soddy floor;
and the music told their shivering hearts
that Spring would come once more.

## Soddy Dug into a Hill

The following poem, *Soddy Dug into a Hill*, is dedicated to Mathias Lorenc (1815-1880), great, great grandfather and Matej Lorenc (Lawrence) (1844-1910), great grandfather. Both were from Damosin, Bohemia; and they came to the United States in 1870. It is also dedicated to Frank Lawrence, grandfather (1874-1967), first baby boy born in Wahpeton, Dakota Territory.

The term "born to this land*" is from a poem of that name by Red Steagall. He used that phrase in a philosophical or metaphorical sense. As to Mathias and Matej Lorenc, that term has literal significance. Until 1848, the rural Czech peasants were serfs of the nobility. As such, they were bound to the land; and if their feudal lord decided to sell it, they went with the land. They could not leave the land or marry someone from a different manor, without their lord's permission. Moreover, their offspring were legally bound to the land and subject to the same restrictions.

Below is a photo of a hillside soddy built in Nebraska in 1880. It was captioned, "*My first house in Nebraska, 1880 Built from "Nebraska brick*". Photography by Solomon Devore Butcher, c. 1886, glass plate negative (6x8). This was a typical hillside soddy.

## *The Soddy Dug Into A Hill*

Looking down on their herd and their family's spread
in the Red River Valley below,
they thought of their ancestral "Greats" and their "Grands",
that lived here a century ago.
It was spoken of yet and they'd never forget
the day of their Grandfather's birth.
He was born to this land! He was born in the land,
in a soddy dug into the earth!

Bohemian settlers! The offspring of serfs,
with transplanted roots in this Red River turf;
with hard-working hands that were well-scarred from toil,
they shoveled a home out of Red River soil.
And there in a hillside, their first child was born,
in the midst of a blizzard's contemptuous scorn.
He was born to the land. He was born in the land-
in a soddy dug into a hill.
Though the years had rolled on and the soddy was gone,
his descendants could picture it still.

With a quilt for a window, a quilt for a door,
and a carpet of straw on a frozen earth floor.
It was cold! It was cold! And the soddy was bare.
Just a table, some chairs and a string bed was there;
with a wood-burning stove that devoured all the wood,
with a voracious greed, just as fast as it could.
It was damp! It was cold, nearly twenty below;
and the winds whipped the quilts and hurled in the snow!

Somehow, he survived and in later years, thrived
in this soddy dug into a hill.
He survived on the strength of a dream and a prayer,
and his family's iron-tough will.
They were born to the land *. He was born in the land,
in a dug-out of tough prairie sod.
Although feverish and weak and ill as a babe,
he was blessed by a merciful God.

His descendants owed much to their "Grands" and their "Greats"—
this sprawling Red River estate.
They could still see them yet; and would never forget.
They were good! They were grand! They were great!
They were born to the land * and gave birth on this land
to descendants who now viewed with pride
this ranch of much worth that the offspring of serfs
transformed out of raw riverside.

# The Gold Rush Widow

Beginning with the California gold rush of 1849, tens of thousands of men left their wives and families in search of gold, land or adventure. And the same is true regarding the wives of cowboys and ranchers who were away from home for months at a time on cattle drives and roundups. Historical records called them grass widows or in the case of wives of gold miners, gold rush widows. Some women didn't wait for their husbands to return, but most rose to the occasion. Some discovered a flair for business, while others held off mortgage and other debt holders, while trying to feed their family. The vast majority of these wives remained behind and kept their homes, homesteads, and businesses intact. Following is a poem about one such wife:

*Prospecting For Gold* by Charles M. Russell (1918)

### *We Had Each Other*

We had each other
though not much more;
but with each other
we were never poor.
With each other,
we were four-fists tough;
and we waged a mighty battle
when times got rough.
We had each other,
and if truth were told,
I wouldn't trade those moments
for a bag a' gold.

I'm a gold-rush widow
outta' Pryor Creek,
but I wish I were the gold dust
that he left to seek.
Prodded by the riches in his
gold-dust dream,
he's out there pannin'
in some Black Hills stream.
He's got gold fever
and the gold dust itch.
"I'm Black Hills bound", he said,
"t' strike it rich."

This drought is troublin'
and the well's near dry.
Gotta haul in water
from the creek nearby.
But I don't mind workin'.
Don't get me wrong.
My shoulder's broad,
and my back is strong.
But the nights are lonely
and the days are grim,
when everything he touched
stirs thoughts of him.

It's a lonely world
and one that's filled with dread
when I lay me down
upon my cold, cold bed.
The wind won't let up
and the sun won't shine
till his head is pillowed
on this bed a' mine;
till his cowboy boots
are standin' two by twos
with this lonely widow lady's
high topped shoes.

We had each other,
and when skies turned gray,
four arms entwined
would drive the clouds away.
With each other,
we were four-fists tough.
We were there together
when the fight got rough.
We held each other—
every care, consoled—
and I wouldn't trade those moments
for a bag a' gold.

# The Last Of The 5000

In the two years after Charley Russell arrived in the Judith Basin area of the Montana territory, the country filled with ranchers and their stock. The area was covered with a mixture of hardy, nutritional grasses. Speculators abounded. At this time Russell was working as a nighthawk for a Horace Brewster; and as such, his duties included the safekeeping of several hundred mounts without the benefit of fences or help from sleeping comrades.

In the winter of 1886-1887, the first cold front hit in November. More storms followed in December. A foot and a half of snow fell between Thanksgiving and Christmas. What little hay they had, most ranchers fed to their horses. In the meantime, the cattle drifted from the frozen high ranges to the bottom land and the sheltered coulees. There was no food there except willows. The first chinook arrived in January, with just enough warming to melt the snow on top. Then it turned cold. On February 3 and 4, one of the worst blizzards in memory set in. The snow crusted. The chinook had succeeded in sealing the ground with a layer of ice, which the cattle hooves could not penetrate. Before he died, Russell dictated to a stenographer this account of what had happened:

> *The winter of '86 and '87 all men will remember. It was the hardest winter the open range ever saw. An awful lot of cattle died. The cattle would go in the brush and hump up and die there. They wasn't rustlers. A horse will paw and get grass, but a cow won't. Then the wolves fattened on the cattle . . . . Now I was living at the OH Ranch that winter. There were several men there, and among them was Jesse Phelps, the owner of the OH. One night, Jesse Phelps had got a letter from Louie Kaufman, one of the biggest cattlemen in the country, who lived in Helena, and Louie wanted to know how the cattle was doing, and Jesse says to me, 'I must write a letter to Louie and tell him how tough it is.' I was sitting at the table with him and I said, 'I'll make a sketch to go with it.' So I made one, a small water color about the size of a postal card, and I said to Jesse, 'Put that in your letter.' He looked at it and said, 'Hell, he don't need a letter, this will be enough.*

On the bottom of a box, Russell completed one of his most memorable paintings. In gray and brown and black colors, he painted a single steer with a Bar R branded on its hip. It was standing in deep snow with horns crooked and eyes hollow. It's backbones and ribs were showing. Wolves lurked in the background; and the steer's tail had been chewed to a nub. The forlorn steer stands lonely and alone. Russell titled it *Waiting For a Chinook (The Last Of the 5000)*.

Louie Kaufman gave the painting to a saddle-maker friend of Russell's, Ben Roberts. Roberts displayed it on the wall of his shop where it collected grime for the next twenty-five years. Eventually, Roberts got the idea of reproducing it; and he printed postcards by the thousands.

*Waiting For a Chinook (The Last Of the 5000).*
Redone by Charlie Russell in the early 1900s
Watercolor re-creation, due to demand for his first popular work in 1886

### *5000 Minus One*

Sibilant and sonorous,
the gentle chinook breeze
hummed along and whistled
as it rustled through the trees;
southeastward down the Rockies,
a tellin' tales of spring;
southeastward, down the Rockies
a smellin' so like spring.
The pity is, the chinook breeze
swept down the slopes too late;
too late to warm and save from harm
a world that couldn't wait.

The range turns cruel and vicious
when entombed beneath the snow;
when a savage blizzard's ragin'
and it's forty-plus below;
and the stock can't find a shelter
'cuz there's just no place t' go;
and the killer winds are slashin'
and it's forty-plus below.
5000 waited for it—
the Chinook that didn't come
and all 5000 perished—
5000 minus one.

The blizzard flung its mortar out
and sepulchered in white
a weary world succumbing to
the blizzard's savage bite.
It clamped its teeth into the herds
of white-man's buffalo,
strugglin' hard to hoof up grass
through ice-encrusted snow.
No food . . . no shelter . . . blizzard gales
a' whippin' cross the land—
the torment was beyond the scope
that man or beast could stand.

5000 waited for it,
a chinook . . . . a ray of sun;
and all 5000 perished—
5000 minus one.
It's temper bared, the blizzard sank
its fangs into their hides;
with not an ounce of pity shown
for suffering stock that died.
The warm Chinook too late exhaled
its thawing, spring-like breath;
too late for herds, all ice-interred,
that kept a date with death.

# MONTANA TERRITORY

After finding gold in the region, Montana became a United States territory (Montana Territory) on May 26, 1864. It was much like a foster child that was shuttled from home to home and then, to yet another home. Montana was originally a part of the Dakota Territory; but through later treaties it became a part of the Washington and then Idaho Territory; while the western section of Montana had previously been a part of both the Oregon and Washington Territories. Montana was admitted to the Union as the State of Montana on November 8, 1889.

To put the time sequence in perspective, the Battle of The Little Bighorn (Custer's Last Stand) occurred in 1876, twelve years after the creation of the Montana Territory and thirteen years before it became a state. Moreover, the Civil War was raging in the states when Montana was admitted as a territory. Why was it admitted as a territory? In 1863, on the eastern slopes of the Rocky Mountains in what was then, Idaho Territory, gold was discovered in a creek by a camp in Alder Gulch. It was the largest placer gold deposit ever discovered; and within a few days, their campsite became Varina, Idaho Territory, and later, Virginia City, Montana Territory. For the Republican administration back in Washington, the preservation of this incredibly strategic gold for the Union cause was essential. In September of that year Sidney Edgerton, arrived in Bannock. He was the person Washington sent to ensure that the gold of Virginia City would support the cause of Abraham Lincoln. Edgerton was later appointed Governor of the Montana Territory.

Thousands of dollars were printed by both the Union and the Confederate governments. These pieces of paper had no backing at all. At the end of the Civil War, the paper money of the South was notoriously worthless, while the Union greenbacks had lost little of their face value. The gold from Virginia City, Montana that persistently flowed into the economy and into the coffers of the Union government, assured the continued value of the greenbacks and their acceptance by industrialists in the North and abroad. The flow of gold mined in Montana into the economy of the North, and the prevention of that flow of gold into the economy of the South became of strategic concern to both president Lincoln and the Union. The gold from Virginia City had a pivotal effect on the economics of the North and its victory. It has been said that "Virginia City gold won the Civil War for the North".

Strategically, it was important to increase the Union minority in the mountain northwest. The Rebel population far outnumbered those with Union allegiance in many areas, particularly in Virginia City and Bannock. To protect the gold, loyal immigrants were needed, as well as loyal authorities for the territories. A territory, of course, was not in the Union. It was a federally owned political unit. It could not secede, but the population could cause problems. The solid loyalty of the population to the South was a problem for the North because of the threat to the Union gold supply. The population was predominantly secessionist and very rebellious about it. They had very little taste for the war "back in the States". But the war had a definite taste for them. That war and both the Union and the Confederacy depended to a very large extent upon the gold that flowed east from Virginia City. The Civil War that was fought in Montana was a vital part of the whole war effort.

The United States Congress often neglected to enact laws for the territories. There were times when there simply was no law in the Idaho and Montana territories. That meant that while the population might have moral objections, they were free to murder, rob or burn another's house down with impunity. And even when there were laws prohibiting it, violence and abuse were rampant. Violence was a part of everyday life in Bannock and Virginia City. Shootings occurred regularly.

A Captain James Liberty Fisk brought two gold nuggets from Alder Gulch to President Lincoln; and he encouraged Lincoln to import emigrants to control the unruly rebels. The Congress acted; they set aside a significant sum to protect emigrants who wished to go from St. Paul to Virginia City. A major portion of the ensuing wagon trains consisted of Republican professionals and merchants. Their arrival began to make a notable difference in the management of the disruptive miners and rebellious secessionists.

A committee of these men held a secret meeting and formed a Vigilance Committee modeled on those formed in California during the 1849 gold rush. All members were sworn to secrecy. After three or four such meetings, the committee grew to about fifty members. By ten days the organization had extended to over a thousand members from an extensive area of the mining country. It was an effective way to fight the Civil War in Montana Territory. A new degree of safety prevailed. The secessionist cause was very quiet, and the territory, with its remarkable and vital flow of gold, was secure for Lincoln. The result was the almost absolute control of the community by the vigilantes. Only outsiders beyond their reach, were able to speak out against them. Their reign triggered one of the deadliest episodes of vigilante justice in American history. During the first five weeks of 1864, while the rest of the nation was preoccupied with the Civil War, a small corps of armed horsemen swept through the mining camps and hanged twenty-one "troublemakers".

But the secessionists had their day. The rebels continued to express that victory for many years, often at their own great cost. Citizens of Virginia City celebrated the assassination of President Lincoln. All over Montana, the Rebels outnumbered and outvoted the Northern Republicans on all kinds of issues. Over all, the Rebel opposition in Montana led to the postponement of statehood for several years. In 1916, the Daughters of the Army of the Confederacy erected a beautiful stone fountain in the Women's Park, directly across from the Civic Center in Helena Montana. This is the farthest north monument to the Confederate army. With this, the Civil War in Montana came to an end.

# Shaney Ridge

Caleb Duncan and his brother George, came to the Montana Territory from New Brunswick, Canada, in the 1870s. (Caleb is my late husband's grandfather.) The following poem, *Shaney Ridge*, is an actual account of what happened to the two brothers after they came to Montana. They were among the first ranchers and settlers in southeast Montana. They first ranched in the Judith Basin area in the vicinity of what is now Lewistown. The poem gives an account of how they built up a large spread in this area and then lost it. Caleb started over on range currently encompassed in Carbon County, Montana. The home base of his ranch was between Roberts and Red Lodge. He obtained a long-term lease on rangeland about fifty miles distant, on the Crow Indian reservation. Up until this ranch was sold in the 1960s, the family drove cattle to and from this range every year. (My late husband figured that he was on at least twenty of these cattle drives.) The name is fictional. All other accounts in the poem are based on actual events. Below is a photo of Caleb Duncan.

## *Shaney Ridge*

They rode into Montana
with their pockets full of poor,
their Appaloosa ponies, and
the homespun clothes they wore.
What was it about Shaney Ridge
that drew the brothers there?
Clear springs of mountain water . . .
they glistened everywhere.

Through icy chills and six foot drifts,
through mud and sleet and mire,
across the range their claim spread out
from Shaney Ridge to Pryor.
None of it was easy.
One crisis spawned another,
but through it all good-natured George
cheered his worried brother.

Winters tortured Shaney Ridge;
but when the sixth one passed,
nature begged forgiveness
and the range thawed out at last.
Caleb's spirit blossomed out
as soon as winter died;
and that spring Caleb left the Ridge
to fetch a promised bride.

When Caleb and his bride returned,
two months had passed them by.
The parching sun was overhead.
The water holes were dry.
The cattle languished on the range;
and George was not around.
As searing as a red-hot brand,
the note that Caleb found.

One night, it seems, that George played cards
with other gambling men.
He lost his cash; his saddle;
he lost his horse . . . . and then,
he bet the spread at Shaney Ridge.
He lost his bet again!
George wrote that he was leaving;
that someday when he'd earn
enough to buy their holdings back,
then only, he'd return.

It took a while for all the words
to really filter through.
But when they did, the pain evoked
each curse that Caleb knew.
The dream called Shaney Ridge was gone;
and Caleb had a bride.
So Caleb started over
and hid the rage inside.
Slowly, slowly, years passed by,
as slowly as his ire;
and just as slow, he gained control
of grazing range near Pryor

What became of brother George?
Caleb never knew.
His bother simply vanished
like Rocky Mountain dew.
Just like the evanescent dew,
impossible to find;
yet when he viewed the Pryor spread,
George often crossed his mind.
He knew he'd chuck the lot of it—
each acre, steer and calf—
just to see George once again
and hear his brother's laugh.

# Empty Cradle Sad

This poem is a true account of an incident involving my late husband's grandmother, Emma Duncan. His father, Robert Leonard Duncan, was the infant that is referred to in the following poem. Below is a photo of Emma Duncan:

***Empty Cradle Sad***

She lovingly beheld her child,
so tender, pink, and sweet.
Her nine-month journey at an end,
Emma felt complete.
For years, she'd waited for him.
Every night she'd pray
that God would make her fertile;
that she'd have a child one day.

Emma thought a women's place
was in that place called home;
that without a child around her,
she'd always feel alone.
For years, though she was grateful
for the loving man she had,
deep inside, the women there
was "empty-cradle sad".

And when at last, she held her child
and clutched him to her breast,
she thought that God was good to her,
that she'd been doubly blest.
Overhead a V of geese
were winging northward bound.
Down below, with seeds and hoe,
Emma sowed the garden ground.

She placed her cradled infant
beneath a pine with care;
hoping, thus, to shield his eyes
from the sun's bright glare.
Now as she hoed her garden,
some motion caught her eye.
She saw a squaw pick up her child,
then swiftly gallop by.

A group of Crows were winding past
along the Dry Creek trail.
They turned around on hearing
Emma's anguished wail.
She flew just like the geese above,
vaulting fence and streams.
Across the range, the air was wracked
with Emma's wrenching screams.

Usually so gentle,
she was vicious . . . savage . . . wild.
She ran and caught the fleeing squaw;
then grabbed her squalling child.
Backing off, the bleeding squaw
fought off a crazed assault;
then lifted up a bloody claw
to urge her foe to halt.

Emma paused; then watched the squaw
ride away alone;
the way she came, was how she left . . . .
without a child . . . alone.
Forgive the Squaw? Impossible!
She knew she never would—
but deep inside, the women there
most surely understood.

# Rustlin' in the Bighorns

Cattle rustling was a problem going back to the earliest days of open range ranching. Rustlers made their living by thieving cattle, altering brands, then selling the cattle for a hefty profit. Stock growers fought back by hiring their own range detectives, taking justice into their own hands, and by working together in stock growers' associations. To thwart them, the cattle rustlers sought out and used remote areas to hide the stolen cattle.

One such rustler, Samuel Garvin, selected a basin in the Bighorn Canyon around 1893. He chose it because of its remoteness . . . but mainly because it was part of the Crow Reservation. While large numbers of cattle ranged there, there was little, if any, law enforcement. The basin was so remote that it took seven years before an agent tracked down Garvin to make him pay the required lease for the land. During that same time Crow cattle were constantly disappearing. Rumors began to circulate that Garvin was involved in rustling cattle. When questioned, Garvin denied any wrongdoing.

In June, 1901, a Grand Jury met in Billings, Montana to decide whether to indict Garvin. It eventually indicted Garvin on six counts. The trial finally opened in Helena in mid-December of 1901. On Christmas Eve the case went to jury. They deliberated through the night, in a room so cold that they could not even sleep. Finally in the late afternoon on Christmas day, the jury produced a verdict of guilty. This was a landmark case, as Garvin and a co-defendant were the first men ever prosecuted and convicted for theft of Crow cattle. Each man was sentenced to a one year in the state penitentiary in Deer Lodge.

Unfortunately this provided only a temporary reprieve from rustling on the Crow reservation. Over the next couple of years the Indian police arrested several different gangs of men who were involved in the theft of Crow cattle and horses. Sentencing was even stiffer for these outlaws, with some getting up to six years in the state prison.

\* \* \* \* \* \* \*

*After graduating from Montana State College, my late husband, Lloyd William "Bill" Duncan, worked for the Bureau of Reclamation. He was the head of an eight man crew that surveyed the Big Horn Mountains, prior to* construction of the Yellowtail Dam. They were deep in the Little Big Horn Canyon for over 4 months. This job, among other things, required them to establish elevations of mountain cliffs down through the canyon. As a consequence, the crew traveled through and over country that very few people had ever seen. They lived chiefly off of the abundant game to be found in the Bighorns at that time. In a very remote section of the Big Horns, the crew came across a narrow pass into the canyon. It had a heavy chain attached to a hook in the granite wall. It was stretched across the pass, and across the adjacent river. Ahead were boulders. The river was boiling with rapids and waterfalls. Past the boulders, there was a pathway to a fertile plateau. It had long been rumored that there was a band of rustlers that operated out of the Big Horn Mountains. They had often been chased . . . but never caught. They always disappeared to the consternation of the nearby Cattlemen's Association.

Who put the chain there? The area was uninhabited by Indians or anybody else, as far as anyone knew. There were many rustlers in the Big Horn Canyon . . . maybe Garvin . . . maybe someone from the Hole In The Wall gang . . . maybe someone else.

### Rustlers' Roost

It long was rumored that a gang a' rustlers hid out there . . .
somewhere in the Bighorns—but none could tell y' where.
They said that way back in those peaks, that gang a' rustlers found-
away from any searching eyes- a stretch a' hidden ground.

I figured it for nonsense . . . . some geezer's windy tale.
I'd never been across it and I'd seen most every trail.
But when I hunted game one day, I came on something strange . . .
a stretch of green, green meadow land up in this mountain range!

Far below, the canyon walls were wet from river spray,
a' kicked up by the rapids as they tossed and boiled away.
On a boulder, overhead, a rifle barrel gleamed;
and what had seemed secluded, wasn't what it seemed.

A group a' rifle totin' men quickly ringed around me,
and motioned me t' walk behind the one a' them that found me.
He led me to a green plateau with knee-high prairie grass.
Who'd a' thought you'd find such range up in this arid pass?

There were elk up in the north end, and mountain goats nearby;
and now and then a ring-necked pheasant shot into the sky.
There were trout down in the river; duck and pheasant, lots 'a game;
and save the river, no way in except the way we came.

And you couldn't raft that river; so what better place t' hide?
You could hole up here forever and never ride outside.
To a man, the gang all said they'd long since known about me;
that though I didn't know of them, they'd seldom been without me.

They'd followed me. They'd searched my tent. They knew each place I went.
They knew I'd been in prison; and about the stretch I'd spent.
They said that they were short a' men and needed one more hand;
that if I'd help with cattle, I was welcome in their band.

They treated me with kindness, and they mostly showed respect;
and though they boozed quite often, they were mostly circumspect.
I'd known so many others on the right side a' the law,
who'd left their mean and bitter barbs a stickin' in my craw.

I stayed and tended to the stock and figured that at least
they weren't as bad as robber barons rustlin' in the East.
The band would often ride away, then later ride on back
without once leaving in their wake a single trace or track.

One Spring, they rustled up a herd and headed for the Chisholm.
Not a one of them returned. They ended up in prison.
They'll be there for a long, long time . . . a good six years or more . . .
but I'll be here a' waitin' . . . if I don't get caught before.

## Goin' For Broke

*The Horse Wrangler Gather'd The Morning Mounts:
'One That Had'n Lived The Life... Couldn't Paint a Picture...
To Please The Eye, of One That Had!'*
(2008), by Bob Coronato. (This painting is courtesy of the Greenwich Workshop, Inc., www.greenwichworkshop.com)

The background in Bob Coronato's painting is similar to the backgrounds that appear in the paintings of Charles M. Russell. Russell was a nighthawk who worked in the area from the Judith Basin to the Pryor Mountains in southeastern Montana. This was about the same time that Caleb and George Duncan were ranching there; and Caleb knew Russell. It was not much of a stretch of the imagination to look at that painting and see Caleb Duncan mounted on his horse during the era of the open range.

During this period, cattle were driven to market or the railroad in late summer. The Union Pacific Railroad was not completed until about 1870. It cut across the Wyoming Territory. During the days of the Open Range and up until the Northern Pacific Railroad was completed in about 1885 as far as the Bozeman Pass, the railroad stop at Casper on the Union Pacific line would have been the closest market/railroad connection to the Montana Judith Basin area. Casper is about four hundred miles from the Judith Basin. It has been estimated that cattle drives traveled at a rate of about ten miles a day. In *Charles M. Russell* by John Taliaferro,1996, Little, Brown & Co. (Canada), it was estimated that it took Charlie Russell, traveling with a wagon and a four-horse team, three weeks to go from Helena to the Judith Basin ( a distance of about 195 miles).

In Bob Coronato's moving painting, the horses are not unduly disturbed by the presence of the wrangler; they seem quite comfortable in his presence. The look and demeanor of the wrangler is that of a caring and kind herdsman who has affection for his herd. What was the wrangler thinking? *Goin' For Broke* is the answer that Coronato's art painted for me.

### *Goin' for Broke*
*(Judith Basin, Montana, 1880)*

That hoof beat staccato!
I cotton the beat.
Let me hear the work sounds
of your range drummin' feet.
Wake up, my four footed,
star chasin' friends.
It's time for my pamperin'
you ponies to end.
The stars have all gone.
It's a sun's peek past dawn.
We're weeks from the railroad;
and late movin' on.

Come alive, you wind racers.
The summer's grown old.
The winds from Alberta
are blowin' in cold.
The winged flocks of wild geese
are passin' us by.
Get fixed for high ridin'.
Get ready to fly.
No lead-footed bangtails
in this wrangler's herd.
Don Pegasus wings
and fly like a bird.

The waddies are waitin'
with bank-notes of beef.
We've trouble enough
so don't give us more grief.
We're six weeks from Casper—
a long way t' go;
and the winds from Alberta
are whisperin' of snow.
We should a left sooner,
of that there's no doubt;
but late summer cloudbursts
left trails flooded out.

This ranchin's a gamble.
Some years things go fine
and some years they don't
which is most of the time.
The cowboys are waitin'.
There's cattle t' drive.
Get a move on you Cayuse!
The dawn's come alive.
You won't get no coddlin'
from this worried Poke.
We're six weeks from Casper
and goin' for broke!

*Cowboy Herding Cattle in the Rain* from *Just A Little Series* (1898) by Charles M. Russell.

## It Cost Me Mary Lou

I listened to the cryin' wind
and felt its cold, cold tears.
The rain, in horizontal slants,
washed off the dusty years.
Once more, I thought of Mary Lou-
the happiness we knew;
and how the cowboy life I loved,
cost me Mary Lou.

Those months out herdin' cattle,
months on end on cattle drives,
with all the cowhands in the crew,
away from home and wives.

With months and months away from her,
and weeks at home, too few,
the wrangler's life this cowboy led-
it cost me Mary Lou.

The coal mine up at Bearcreek,
the copper mines at Butte,
I tried. My God, I tried 'em,
but my loathing was acute.
I missed the scent of prairie sage
and hearin' cattle bawl;
I missed the roundups, cattle drives,
the range, I missed it all.
I tried t' fit in elsewhere,
but wranglin's all I knew;
and much as I loved cowboy life,
it cost me Mary Lou.

Now as Autumn runs its course,
and frigid Winter nears,
I listen while the moaning wind
cries floods of lonely tears.
They're peltin' down from dismal clouds
of dark and gloomy hue,
as I recall how cowboy life
cost me Mary Lou.
The copper mines, I loathed 'em,
and the coal mines? Loathed 'em too,
and couldn't take 'em anymore.
It cost me Mary Lou.

# STATE OF MONTANA

Montana became a state on November 8, 1889, with Helena as the capital. But Butte soon emerged as the industrial giant of the state. Butte began as a gold camp. Hard-rock mining had begun in the 1880s, but shaft mining commenced when vast deposits of copper were discovered there. Butte subsequently became known as the Richest Hill on Earth, and the world's largest smelter was built at nearby Anaconda. The so-called War of the Copper Kings, was won by Marcus Daly, whose Anaconda Company became one of the largest mining conglomerates in the world. The company smashed the mining unions, influenced the state legislature, acquired almost all of Montana's daily newspapers, and virtually controlled the state for three-fourths of a century.

Cattle and sheep grazing in Montana started in the 1860s, when herds were driven overland from Texas. The vast grasslands seemed ideal for cattle, but a severe winter in 1886-87 almost wiped out the herds.

The Homestead Act was presented to Lincoln and was signed into law on May 20, 1862. By this time, of course, the nation was over a year into the Civil War. The secession of the Southern states gave the passage of the act a political angle as well, in that it would benefit the United States to have as many free settlers as possible in the western territories.

Under this law, any man or woman who was twenty-one years old or the head of a family could have 160 acres of undeveloped land by living on it for five years and paying $18 in fees. However, they were also required to build a home, make improvements and farm the land before they could own it outright. Alternatively, the homesteader could purchase the land for $1.25 per acre after having lived on the land for six months. Homesteaders began pouring in to bust the sod and attempt to grow grain on the largely semiarid land that was not irrigated.

*Commemorative stamp, below.* (Note the soddy.)

# That Pretty Patch of Green

*Last Chance or Bust* by Charles Russell (1900)

### *Westward Ho, The Wagons Rolled*

Stark and primitive, it loomed
in wild, primeval glory;
no province yet, this land they trod,
but just a territory.
They wondered in the wilderness,
assailable, alone;
a planet-breadth away
from all the world they'd ever known;
a land so rawboned . . . . rugged . . . .
that the states back East seemed tame.
Common sense said, "Turn around!
Go back from where y' came."

Then echoed back a sun bleached skull
that leered up from the range,
"This land's not meant for such as you
too merciless and strange.
Just look around . . . . there's no place here

for fools the likes a' you.
This land'll break those hearts a' yours
before your journey's through."
Then from the orbits that were eyes,
there slithered out a snake.
It warned them, "Better men than you,
this land's been known t' break."

But then, beyond the arid waste,
beyond the skulls that leered,
beyond the hoary scrags of sage,
a patch of green appeared.
A verdant stretch of meadow grass,
a tonic sip of green,
and Westward Ho . . . their spirits soared
and raised their sagging dream.
A waving stand of knee-high hope
on which their dream could graze;
a vision there of things to come
on which their eyes could gaze.
Westward Ho, their wagons rolled
through terrors yet unseen,
driven by the promise of
that pretty patch of green.

# Memories Of Alvin Wolf

*(Before he died, my father, Alvin D. Wolf, taped a record of his life from early childhood on. This record was transcribed; and it now appears in a lovely hard cover book, The Descendants of Gottlieb Wolf (1833-1880) et al. This book was compiled by my sister, Dolores McMullen; and it was published by her as a gift to family members in 2006. The book was the culmination of thirty-five years of genealogical research. The following data was taken from this book. The photos were found in family scrapbooks she compiled.)*

My grandfather, Hermann Wolf (1866-1949) immigrated to the United States when he was 16 years old. He lived with relatives in Wisconsin for awhile and worked in logging camps and lumber woods. Later, he moved to Minnesota, where he farmed and raised work horses that he eventually sold to the railroad. Hermann personally delivered the horses to Montana via rail. In 1909, he filed for a homestead on land located in Osborne, Montana. It wasn't much of a town, just a store and a post office. (Osborne no longer exists; it is a part of the Huntley Project.) While located there, my grandfather farmed, but the major part of his income was probably derived from freighting logs from the Bull Mountains for the railroad. In his tape, my father said this:

"Dad always had good horses. In Minnesota during the summertime, he would farm and then take horses to Montana. At that time, the railroad company would haul the horses free of charge. They used the horses to help build the railroads. The ones Dad helped build were the Milwaukee around Osborne and the line that goes from Laurel to Great Falls, MT. Logs were hauled from the Bull Mountains to build timber bridges.

When they were freighting, they would first start out across the country at night. When they stopped they'd feed the horses. Indians were till roaming around the country then. Although we never had any problems with them, at night we'd worry about losing our horses. There was a lot of deer around; and hunters were sent out to get meat for the men."

Above is a picture of grandfather Hermann, and his oldest child and my uncle, Berthold Wolf (1897-1918). They were pictured with some of their stock, a four horse team. Bert appeared to be about twelve in this photo; so the photo was probably taken around 1909.

Below is a picture of Uncle Bert and my grandfather, pitching hay to cattle from a wagon. Bert appeared to be around sixteen or seventeen; so the photo was probably taken around 1913.

Below is a picture of my grandmother, Emma Gerlach Wolf (1875-1960), and my father, Alvin D. Wolf (1909-1991). Dad was the second baby boy born in Huntley Project. The photo shows them feeding chickens in front of the log chicken house. The family home and barn were made from timber hauled in from the Bull Mountains. The barn was built first. While the house was being built, the family lived in the barn. (The house was still standing until about five years ago, when it burned down.)

About my grandmother, Dad said this:

*"Mother had a big job. She raised a big family and she worked hard. The women of today don't know what work is. Everything in those days had to come out of the garden. You raised your own food and that was the women's job. All the clothes you had were washed on the washboard. You had to carry your own water from the well and carry your own wood in for the stoves. You didn't turn the faucet on to get hot water. When they washed clothes, they put a boiler on to heat the water. They then took care of the garden. It was a tremendous job, and I don't know how they ever got their work done.*

*We never were out of clean clothes. We always had better home-cooked food than you get at home today. Milking cows usually turned out to be the women's job twice a day. They had kerosene lamps and one had to see that they were filled all the time. The chimneys had to be kept clean as they would smoke up and get black. How did she ever get her work done?*

*Mom always had quite a few people to cook for, not only for her family, because we usually had hired men around. Breakfast was usually at six or six-thirty. Meals were regular and on time and you didn't fool around. Twelve o'clock or noon was dinner-time and you were there! Between six and six-thirty was supper and again, you were there or you didn't get any! This was every day...."*

The following picture (probably taken about 1914) shows Uncle Bert and my father when he was about five years old. They are pictured on family saddle horses. Bert was my grandfather's right-hand man from the time he was a young boy. (His death while in the army during WWI in 1918, about four year after this picture was probably taken, was a heartbreaking loss.)

About horses, my father said this:

*"In Osborne where I was born, I used to ride horses all the time. I guess I was born in the saddle. I remember the first time I ever got thrown off a horse. Dad set me on a colt and then clapped his hands. The colt bucked me off. I couldn't have been more than four at the most. The reason I remember this so well is that I landed on a manure pile but I didn't get hurt. That little colt was killed by the railroad. She got in front of a train.*

*... When you're seven or eight years old, you could drive a team of horses and go out and mow hay in those days. I would go out on my saddle horse and bring the milk cows home. The cows were in the hills for grass. Of course, the horse did more than I did and knew what she was doing more than I did."*

Below is a photo of Aunt Agnes Wolf Burnstead (1878-1997). It shows Agnes on the horse to the left. (I don't know who the other rider is.) When Uncle Bert died in 1918, Agnes took his place and did everything on the place but irrigate. She was a very hard working, intelligent woman, typical of the many women of the West who took over farms and ranches when their husbands were absent.

The following picture shows the Wolf family in their old Model T Ford. It was taken in front of their Osborne home. Seated on the running board are Grandpa and Agnes. My father, Al, is peering over their shoulder, and Grandma is standing toward the front of the car. The picture was probably taken around 1915.

Grandpa filed his Final Proof of Homestead Entry in 1914; and in 1915, he sold the Osborne homestead. In 1916 he purchased about 650 acres of land in Stillwater Country, Montana from the Northern Pacific Railroad. This land was located west of Park City near a railroad stop, then known as Rapids. In his taped account, my father said this:

*"Dad sold the place in Huntley (Osborne) and bought a place outside of Park City... He had one of the nicest farms in the whole country. It was about half way between Park City and Columbus. The land was located on both sides of the railroad. The grazing land was on the north side of the road and the farm land was on both sides.... The Stub was a train that ran from Billings to Butte. When it went by, we'd wave. That was the only thing we had to look at, and you could set your clock by it. He would stop and pick up our milk and cream and take it to the Livingston or Billings creamery. The money from the cows, chickens and butter was your grocery money. Whenever flour was needed, we'd take a load of wheat to town in Park City and trade it for flour and bran for the calves....*

*The trains were your only means of transportation for any distance. They didn't have roads like we do today. There was nothing but dirt roads and you didn't even have a gravel road. You would go into town once a week unless you broke down. In the winter, it would be even longer. One didn't have radios, telephones, or daily newspapers. You could be in war for several weeks and you wouldn't know it unless someone told you. The only means of communication was from mouth to mouth or the Columbus newspaper that came out once a week. When you were in town, you would listen to all the news and tell everyone. Once in awhile we'd get the newspaper from the Stub."*

In the two pictures below, you can see the old farmhouse that Grandpa built. I was born there in 1930. In the first photo, Grandpa and Grandma are standing by the porch. In the second photo, Agnes is standing by the side of the house with her horse. The house is still standing, but the new owners have built a larger house that is more to their liking; and our dear old house is decaying with neglect.

The following picture shows the barn that Grandpa built. It is still in excellent condition. When Grandpa had it, the family brand was painted on the front below the roof. On the bottom side of the photo, you can see the edge of the Big Ditch, used for irrigation. The Yellowstone River was close by to the south.

Dad is pictured in the two photos below. In the first one, he is standing by the porch with his dog and his Remington rifle. In the second, he is standing in front of his horse. His gun can be seen sticking out of a leather case attached to his saddle. In the background is a deserted boarded-up barn with a sagging roof, location unknown. There are many like it that dot the Montana prairies. These two photos were probably taken around 1921 and 1924. Concerning horses, Dad made an interesting comment:

*"We had horses that were just as good fisherman as we were. We would fish right off the horse. They knew every hole in the river. They'd go right up to the spot to fish and as soon as that fish was on the line, they'd back right up to the shore. That was an easy way to fish. You didn't have to walk much."*

The final picture below shows Uncle Bert shortly before he died in the service in 1918. It shows him holding a goose in one hand and his rifle in the other. It is significant that the few pictures of Dad and Uncle Bert I have show them with rifles. Guns have always played a dominant role in Montana.

The West we enjoy today was built with the sweat and sacrifice of men and women like my relatives. Montana cattle were (and maybe still are) highly prized by Midwestern farmers and feedlots because they would survive while other livestock would languish or die. In the same way, the people of the West were unique—more independent, self reliant, and imbued with a rock-hard inner strength. They were survivors that sacrificed blood and sweat to overcome severe hardships.

## The Men from Way Out West

In the words of another poem, "You can always tell an eastern dude", I used to hear them say. "It's not the way he looks or talks. He thinks a different way." There is a unique quality about the men from the west... independent, resourceful, with a rock-hard inner strength. And if it had been otherwise, they would not have tamed the West... the West would have tamed or broken them.

*Cutting Out* by N. C. Wyeth (1904).

### *The Men From Way Out West*

It wasn't their genetics
or some fabled cowboy deed.
Their rock-hard ranch existence
had spawned a different breed;
a different breed-a different creed-
a different style of life-
a different way of coping
and overcoming strife.

Much, much different men emerged
distinct from all the rest;
more sage and cactus in their guts,
the men from way out west.
It wasn't how they walked or talked
or how the cowboys dressed.
They'd be one in a business suit
while on some Wall street quest.
And it was more than how they roped,
or how the men could ride.
Their rock-hard ranch existence
had branded them inside.

So deep inside the brand was burnt,
it set the men apart—
more inner strength, more stamina,
more steely grit and heart;
just like Montana cattle,
livestock that survived
when lesser stock all languished
or dropped somewhere and died.
It wasn't their genetics
or some fabled cowboy deed.
Their rock-hard ranch existence
had spawned a different breed.

# She Talked with Horses

***Dedicated to Agnes Wolf Burnstead (1878-1997), pictured below.*** Her daughter told me that she taught her horse many tricks after seeing Cody's Wild West show. In his memories, my father, Alvin Wolf, also talks of seeing this show. (Cody, Wyoming is less than one hundred miles from where they lived.)

Both she and my grandfather were exceptional equestrians who loved horses. It is significant that she was with a horse in nearly all of the photos I have of her when she was a young woman. When she was young and living on the ranch, she probably had far more contacts with horses than with friends of her age. They didn't have nice oiled or even graveled roads back then. Visits with friends and relatives were, more than likely, limited. The family would go into town on Saturday—provided the dirt road wasn't snowed over or a ribbon of mud. In other words they went into town or visited friends and neighbors sporadically. The horses, she saw every day; and she did have exceptional equestrian abilities.

### *She Talked With Horses*

"She talks with horses", folks would say.
Hyperbole, I guessed.
Yet, when it came to handling them,
she was about the best.
More than just a rancher's daughter,
western born and bred;
she handled horses like a pro,
and those that knew her said
that she could outride those who rode
in Cody's Wild West Show.
She interacted with a horse
like few that Cody'd know.

She talked with horses like few folks.
She knew each word they said.
Her mind met theirs and they communed,
two kindred souls instead.
She talked to them with heart in hand.
They heard each word she spoke.
They heard it in her gentle hands,
and knew each word she'd stroke.
Her heart had ears that listened;
and the words were plain and clear.
Their was no word the horses spoke,
her heart's ears didn't hear.

She often thought about the scope
of God's eternal plan;
and she was never one who thought
that God just favored man.
God must have loved them too, she thought,
the same way he loved her;
and God in his benevolence
blessed both of them, for sure.
She talked with horses, soul to soul;
and cared what horses thought.
That's why she talked with horses,
when other folks could not.

## Dust, Grasshoppers, and Drought!

With the onset of World War I, the demand for wheat was mind-boggling; and farmers were paid record prices. It made sense to cultivate every inch of the land. During the war, the Great Plains produced millions and millions of bushels of wheat and corn, which helped to feed America as well as numerous nations overseas. But eventually, the popular farming practices that made the plains so productive were beginning to take a toll on the land. Native grassland was replaced with heavily disked fields of straight, deeply plowed row crops. During the years when there was adequate rainfall, the land produced bountiful crops. However, as a drought that started in the early 1930s persisted, the farmers kept plowing and planting with increasingly dismal results. The decade opened with prosperity and growth. But in the summer of 1931, the rain simply stopped.

The water level of lakes dropped by five feet or more. The wind picked up the dry soil that had nothing to hold it down. Great black clouds of dust began to blot out the sun. In some places, the dust drifted like snow, darkening the sky for days, covering even well-sealed homes with a thick layer of dust on everything. Dust storms engulfed entire towns. It had taken a thousand years for Nature to build an inch of topsoil on the land, but it took only minutes for one good wind to sweep it all away.

The primary impact area of the Dust Bowl, as it came to be known, was on the Southern Plains. The Northern Plains weren't so badly affected, but the drought, dust, and agricultural decline were felt there as well. Nevertheless, farmers kept on plowing, hopeful that the rains would return in a matter of days, or perhaps months. In the spring of 1934, the massive drought impacted 27 states severely and affected more than 75 percent of the country. It was the worst drought in U.S. history. Drought was nothing new to the farmers in the Dakotas, Montana, and Wyoming. Since their fathers and grandfathers had settled there, there had been dry periods interspersed with times of sufficient rainfall. But the drought that descended on them in 1931 was more severe than most could remember. Four years of drought shriveled the crops and left the loose top soil to the mercy of the ever-present winds.

On Sunday, April 14, 1935, (Black Sunday), a massive front moved across the Great Plains from the northwest. Packing winds of 60 miles per hour, the loose topsoil was scooped up and mounded into billowing clouds of dust hundreds of feet high. People hurried home, for to be caught outside could mean suffocation and death. The dust and darkness halted all forms of transportation and the fine silt sifting through any crack or joint forced the closure of hospitals, flour mills, schools and businesses.

The Dust Bowl of the 1930s lasted about a decade. Its primary area of impact was on the southern Plains. While the northern Plains were not so badly affected, nevertheless, the drought, windblown dust and agricultural decline were no strangers to the north. Montana and Wyoming did not escape the horrors of the dust bowl. For a time, the weather was kind. For example, in 1916, Shelby, Montana received more than 15 inches of rain; but in 1919, after three years of drought, the town received less than 7 inches of rain. The drought continued and was coupled with high winds and grasshoppers. Range fires that destroyed crops, were frequent.

In their desperation, Montana farmers imported over a hundred thousand turkeys to eat the grasshoppers. The turkeys thrived . . . but so did the grasshoppers! An account of the severe drought and dust storms in Montana by Lorna Thackeray appeared in the Billings Gazette. She quoted Alfred Hirsch, who then lived at Kinsey, Montana:

> *Horses struggling to survive on desiccated range north of Miles City wandered around hairless during the worst years of the Great Depression. "They would eat the tails off each other—and the manes, too. . . . Desperate livestock gnawed on the fence posts for what little moisture remained in the wood. Sometimes, grasshoppers got to the wood first. Sometimes dust blown in from dry cropland covered the fence posts so deep even the grasshoppers couldn't get to them.*

During the beginning of the Depression and The Dust Bowl, I lived on my grandfather's ranch where I was born. It was located near Park City, Montana. My parents later farmed near Joliet, Montana, but couldn't make it because of the severe drought. They moved to Billings, Montana where my father found work at a lumber yard.

## Black Sunday
*April 14, 1935*

Black Sunday, nineteen thirty-five . . .
the day turned into night;
the thick, black dust that plagued us
had blotted out the light.
It looked like some satanic hand
had poured tar from on high.
It blew and boiled above us,
and charred the raging sky.
Armageddon? Some believed it-
that an awful, evil spell
had been cast upon creation
by the anti-Christ from hell.

The Prairie's crust,
gust after gust,
was blown to God knows where.
Outside the house-
Inside the house-
dust clogged the heavy air.
Black Sunday . . . . All who saw it
could clearly understand
that crops would never grow again
upon the ravaged land.
Armageddon? Some believed it-
but the rest knew all too well . . . .
call it what you want to,
it was a living hell.

The cruel winds blew incessantly
and stripped the prairie bare.
The precious soil, thus swept aloft,
tarred black the heavy air.
We went outside with goggles;
and on faces, towels were hung.
Still dust filmed the eyes and nose,
and grit begrimed the tongue.
Dust filtered through the smallest cracks
and settled on the floors;
upon the stove and in the food;
and even in the drawers.
Everywhere . . . dust everywhere . . .
dirty sheets of silt,
although we dusted, swept and mopped
and battled to the hilt.

"Would this nightmare never end?",
we asked—but knew full well,
that even when Black Sunday waned,
we'd still be facing hell.
Neighbors . . . some already gone-
just like the dust clouds, blown
down some dust-filled highway
to places yet unknown.
And what of us? Where would we go?
How could we leave our home . . .
just leave the only life we'd known . . .
just pack it up and roam?
Oh, the dreams—all dashed to dust . . . .
and hopes that wind did quell;
no golden fields of wheat for us-
just bitter grains of hell!

# The Depression Years in Montana

The Great Depression that affected the entire nation, began in 1930. However, the depression, per se, hit Montana in the so called boom-years of the roaring 20s. After World War I, a severe drought in Montana, coupled with an international decline in farm prices produced a serious economic crisis. This led to the end of the homesteading boom. Instead, it signaled the beginning of a twenty-year drought that was accompanied by wind, dust, grasshoppers . . . and poverty. The agricultural boom turned into a bust.

The old-timers knew that cycles of drought are a natural part of the Montana climate. Unfortunately, many homesteaders were unaware of this reality. The drought began in 1917; and by 1919, Montana endured one of the most calamitous year in the state's history. The drought spread across the state, even into the normally well-watered valleys of the western mountains. High winds set in during the 1920s, whipping away great clouds of pulverized topsoil. The wind produced hideous dust storms similar to those that decimated so much of the southern Great Plains a decade later.

As if this were not enough, market prices for agricultural products dropped drastically. By 1920, as Europe recovered from WW I, it cut back on the purchase of U.S. farm commodities. U.S. agricultural prices dropped sharply. Wheat which had sold for $4.20 per bushel in August, 1920, fell to $1.25 per bushel in October, 1921. Farmers also faced light harvests because of the severe drought. Where Montana farmers had been accustomed to yields of 25 bushels to the acre, they averaged a scant 2.4 bushels per acre in 1919. In 1920 they were hit by yet another bad crop year. Many Montana farmers faced the future without adequate means of support. Wagons and jalopies rolled out of Montana with mattresses and belongings tied to their sides. Occasionally a grimly sardonic message would appear, such as, "Goodbye, Old Dry!"

Between 1919 to 1925, roughly 2 million acres passed out of production; and about 11,000 farms, or about 25% of the state's total number of farms, were vacated. About 20,000 mortgages were foreclosed and about half of Montana's farmers left their land. It has been estimated that 60,000 people left Montana. In 1914, a state promotion publication urged prospective settlers to hurry because in a short time the "free" homestead would be but a memory of the past. But in 1921, a state document tried to turn would-be settlers away by pointing out that no "good" homestead opportunities were to be found in the state.

Montana was the only state of the 48 to lose population during the "prosperous" roaring 20s. Moreover, Montana had the highest bankruptcy rate in the nation during this decade.

# Makin' Do . . . .
# A Great Depression Remembrance

*Migrant Mother* by Dorothea Lange (1936) for U.S. Farm Security Administration. (She has been called the greatest photographer of the Depression era.)

### *Makin' Do*

Momma was a waitress;
and one thing that she knew
was prayin' hard t' God above
t' help her just make do.

My coat was Uncle Henry's
before Ma cut it down;
and the little kids had dresses
made from Momma's wedding gown.

We had a lotta home-baked bread,
and lots a Momma's stew.
We next-t'-never had a roast,
'cuz we wuz makin' do.

Our cousins all had horses,
and we begged t' have one too;
but we could barely feed our cow,
and we wuz makin' do.

Momma said she "couldn't hardly
make the two ends meet";
and "we didn't need no pony
cuz we had a pair a feet".

She didn't heed our moans at all.
She plumb ignored our groans;
and makin' do was drilled into
the marrow of our bones.

We didn't have a lot back then
but few folks had much more,
cuz back in those Depression times,
most everyone was poor.

I'm grateful now for many things,
and I give Mom her due;
I'm grateful that she taught her kids
the art of makin' do.

## **Field Of Dreams**

Hard times in Montana-
that seemed to be the norm.
At least that's all I ever knew
from the moment I was born.
But that all changed with World II;
the country needed wheat,
beef and beans and tons of wheat,
and tons of sugar beets.

All across Montana, ranchers like
John Mohr
planted crops on pasture land
they'd never cropped before.
John Mohr's lower forty
was planted with seed beans.
Eventually, this bean field
became my "field of dreams".

Hard times in Montana
Were harder, far, for some . . .
some on the dole, or WPA
and some were on the bum.
A thirteen year old hopeful,
I searched the town around.
10 cents an hour for tending kids;
that's all I ever found.

But that all changed with John Mohr's
beans.
Mohr was hiring local teens.
50 cents an hour he paid . . .
and ten hours every day.
I hoed the beans in John Mohr's field-
a dreaming all the way.
Ten hours a day of bending down,
And hoeing through a row;
attacking weeds at every step,

and brandishing my hoe.
But I was busy dreaming
about the dough I'd make;
too full of dreams to care if my
poor aching back would break.

I hoed a million weedy rows.
With every ache I swore,
"No more will I wear worn out
clothes . . .
I'm sick of being poor.
This year I'll wear a rich girls clothes
for all the school to see . . . . .
for when I get my pay from Mohr,
that rich girl will be me."

I've climbed a long way since those
days,
but memory sees me poor.
And no check's ever meant as much
as what I got from Mohr.
The rancher made a profit.
The soldiers got some beans.
And that year, I was duded up
Just like the high school queens.

# Earl Durand—The Mountain Man

*Pictured above*: Earl Durand.
(This photo is from an old 1939 newspaper clipping.)

As a child during the '30s, I walked home from school at noon, for lunch. Nearly all my classmates did the same. All of the family was home for a hot meal; and we ate at the table together. The radio, however, was sometimes the focus of our attention. One bulletin that we waited for anxiously was the latest news about Earl Durand. Some folks called him the Tarzan of the Tetons; and others, the Robin Hood of the Rockies. He was a true woodsman and mountain man, on that most people agreed. To some he was somewhat of a folk hero whom they had compassion and sympathy for, if not admiration. To others, he was a joke and a criminal. But some facts are indisputable.

He was a remarkable athlete about six-feet-two inches, weighing close to two hundred pounds (none of which was fat). He ran miles every day; and it was said that he could cover forty miles at night at a lope. He lived in the mountains from April through October, keeping himself alive with his gun, his knife and his wits. Durand wasn't completely opposed to eating meat cooked, but he preferred it raw. During the winter months, he lived in a wall tent behind his parent's home. Durand had difficulty remaining enclosed in rooms for any length of time. He kept a kerosene stove burning in his tent when it got cold; but he became used to a chill that would be intolerable to most people. One young teenage neighbor who used to hunt antelope with Durand, Dick Smith, said, *"He felt trapped, stifled when he was inside buildings for more than a few minutes. He hadn't slept inside his parent's home since he was sixteen."* (I've heard of people suffering panic attacks during MRI scans . . . but this has got to be about the most severe case of claustrophobia on record. I remember those winters in Montana when it hit 40 degrees below zero . . . . so cold it hurt to breath . . . and he was outside of his parents' home in a tent. Imagine the state of mind of that individual in a jail cell.)

In 1939, he was arrested and jailed for poaching elk, resisting arrest, and for killing a rancher's calf. He was sentenced to six months and jailed for the poaching while he awaited sentencing for the theft of the calf. During his incarceration, Deputy Riley taunted Durand, telling him that he'd get twenty years in the state pen; and that he'd forget what the mountains looked like by the time he got out. Cody lawyer, Millard R. Simpson ( later governor and Wyoming senator), said that Durand used to stand close to the cell door glowering, holding the bars tight while Riley taunted him.

Two days later, he escaped the Cody jail by assaulting a deputy with the milk bottle taken from a dinner tray that the deputy was bringing him. He forced the deputy to drive him to his parents' home in nearby Powell. Durand shot and killed a deputy sheriff and town marshal in the driveway of his parents' home. For ten days, he eluded arrest by fleeing to the mountains. He killed two members of the sheriff's posse tracking him. Montana mobilized its National Guard and a sheriff's posse; but they failed to flush him out of hiding. He had already escaped by carjacking the posse's radio operator and forcing him to drive him back to Powell.

Once in Powell, he went to the First National Bank to rob it. During the course of the robbery he began to shoot out the windows of the bank which alerted the local residents who took up armed positions outside the bank. Durand tied up the bank president and two other bank employees and forced them to walk out of the bank in front of him. One of the three hostages was shot and killed by the volley of bullets that met them at the door. Durand returned their fire. In the door of a gas station cross the street from the bank, a seventeen-year-old high school student fired on Durand. The bullet hit Durand in the chest and knocked him off his feet. He crawled back into the lobby of the bank where he managed to shoot himself.

Opinions vary as to the character of Durand—folk hero or villain. The foregoing poem does not purport to set out all of actual facts but only to try to capture the character of Earl Durand as I perceived it to be, at the time. (I was then about nine years old.)

### *The Mountain Man*
*The Legend of Earl Durand*

The mountain moon's a ridin'
on the stallion of the night;
with snowflakes softly glidin' down
its flowing mane of light.
The midnight winds are siftin'
through the driftin' flakes of snow;
and you can hear 'em whistlin'
through the pine trees as they blow

Some think my trail's a lonely one,
without a soul in sight;
with no one there t' talk to
save the wailin' winds of night.
But what I am's a mountain man.
I do jus' fine out here.
I've mostly slept beneath the sky.
I feed on elk and deer.

Good friends, these mountains are t' me,
the kindest ones I've known;
and when I'm in these mountains,
I 'm never quite alone.
I like t' hear the whisperin'
of a gentle mornin' breeze;
and listen t' the birdsong
that's pourin' from the trees

A posse's out there after me
with bullets by the score.
But they won't take this mountain man
the way they did before.
I've gotta keep on ridin' now,
and hidin' from the law
avoiding men, evading them—
holed up in some dark draw.
I killed game outta season,
but the reason for my plight
is, when they jailed me, I escaped,
and killed while during flight.

I couldn't breath. I couldn't think.
Went crazy in that cell.
It stripped me of my reason,
and delivered me t' hell.
No longer was I human,
but an animal confined,
without the human faculties
that bless the human mind.

A mountain man is what I am,
unfettered, wild and free;
and nevermore will prison bars
mock the man in me.
Nor will they hang this mountain man.
Of this I'm sure for I've
resolved that they will never take
this mountain man alive.

And when their bullets find me,
as their bullets surely will,
a free, unfettered mountain man
is what they're gonna kill.
The mountain moon's a ridin'
on the stallion of the night;
with snowflakes softly slidin' down
its silvery tail of light.
When I am dead and buried
and this flight from terror ends,
I'll mount that coal-black stallion
and rejoin my mountain friends.

# The Red Lodge Rodeo

*Bill Linderman (pictured above)* was tabbed the original "King" of professional rodeo by his peers. He won seven world titles during his career in three different events; and he was all-around world champion in 1950 and 1953. In 1950, Linderman accomplished something no cowboy has done since. He won world titles at both ends of the arena, in steer wrestling and saddle bronc riding.

### Red Lodge on July the 4th
### (1940s-1950s)

Forget? I've not forgotten
those times when I was young;
and the memory of those rodeos
tastes sweet upon my tongue.
Red Lodge on July the fourth—
I'd find a way to go
to where the crowd and action was,
the home town rodeo.

I'd head on out for Red Lodge
where everyone was goin';
where rodeo grounds were packed with folks
and streets were over flowin.

The ruckus of the rodeo
would rock the Red Lodge crowd.
The cheers and chants and jeers and rants
would vibrate thunder-loud.

And when the chute was opened
and Bud Linderman shot out,
the home town crowd went crazy,
as the bronco spun about.
With both legs on the same side,
he'd spur the bronc's right side . . .
then toss across to the left,
a spurrin' as he'd ride.
The right side . . . then the left side . . .
a spurrin' all the while;
and then he'd face the hometown crowd
and flash his hometown smile.

And when it came Turk Greenough's time,
we'd marvel at his skill;
the way he'd step right off the bronc
like it was standin' still.
Standin' still? Not hardly!
It bucked! It kicked! It spun!
But Turk stepped off so casual-like
when his ride was done.

And then came destiny's fair child,
and I can see him still—
the—champion all 'round cowboy—
Bud's big brother, Bill.
He could ride the bulls and broncs
that came straight outta hell.
He could ride most any brute
and always he'd excell.

Rodeos . . . I've seen a lot,
but nothin' can compare
to the home town rodeo
when all your friends are there;
and you're all there together
a cheerin' loud; and when
the riders that you're cheerin' for
are local home town men.

## 8 Seconds From Glory

He mounted the bull; and at blast-off he swore
he wouldn't be cast off like dung anymore.
Let Hell explode! He was bolted astride;
and this was the day for an 8 second ride.
Let the bull hurtle and rocket through space,
propelled by its hate for the whole human race.
He'd ride out each frenzied eruption and spin.
This journey was his. It was his day to win!

8 seconds from glory! 8 seconds from fame!
8 seconds away from the crowd's wild acclaim!
Just 5 seconds more . . . he refused to be thrown.
Just 5 seconds more, and the buckle he'd own.
Though his frame throbbed like jets
from the thrust of the blast,
he hunkered down tight
till some three seconds passed.

2 seconds from glory . . . just 2 seconds more!
He'd ride the full 8 or die trying, he swore!
But glory's elusive. It's here, then it's gone.
One moment, it's yours . . . . and the next, it's withdrawn.
With 1 second more . . . just a second to go,
the darn bull exploded and stole the blamed show.

\* \* \*

Glory is fleeting. It seldom lasts long;
and his glory vanished like dew drops at dawn.

During WWII, the ranching/farming communities in the West were emptied of men and older boys. They were in the armed forces serving their country. Families placed silk banners in their windows, displaying with pride blue stars for servicemen currently serving and gold stars for servicemen killed in the war. There were very few windows in the West that didn't have a banner with at least one blue star on it. This poem is dedicated to Lloyd William Duncan (1925-2002), pictured below.

## Cowboys Don't Cry

When I was a kid growin' up in the West,
most times I wore boots and my fringed leather vest.
When grade school was out and summer came 'round,
most days I'd hang out on the rodeo ground.
With my ten gallon hat, this kid looked right smart,
a ten year old cowboy dressed up for the part.

I remember that year on the fourth of July
a cracker popped off in my face near an eye.
A medic came out. I remember him well.
He bandaged a face that was hurtin' like hell.
It burned like I'd doused it with Momma's strong lye;
but the white-coated medic said, "Cowboys don't cry!"

So I clenched my teeth, and stood straight and tall;
'cuz I was a cowboy and cowboys don't bawl.
And from that day on, I never once cried;
not even when Caleb, my Granddaddy, died.
The World War was ragin' when I was fifteen;
and I joined the Army when I turned eighteen.

I was lucky in Leyte, Medora, Luzon
but ran out of luck when we beached at Bataan.
With a soul that was shell-shocked, I saw Hell explode
as a beach of God's finest, the strafing planes mowed.
I dove from the horror that hailed from the sky,
and I thought of the man that said, "Cowboys don't cry!"

As I saw my buddy's blood pool on the ground,
from his torn shreds of flesh I could hear not a sound.
I fear the best part of me died in that war.
The cocky, tough cowboy I was, was no more.
With eyes that were screaming and no longer dry,
I scoffed at the man that said, "Cowboys don't cry!"

The bullet-strafed ground was stained dirty red;
and was littered with bodies of buddies now dead.
Satan's mad demons, I met them that day—
I saw what Hell looked like. I learned how to pray.
With fists clenched in fury, I shook at the sky;
and I cursed the damn fool that said, "Cowboys don't cry!"

While much has been written about the prairies and rangeland of the original Dakota Territory, its crowning glory was, and is, the lofty mountain ranges that pierce the sky. The following verse was written for Rocky Mountain man, Howard F. Barber. He was born, grew up and ranched in the heart of the Rockies. While currently in a nursing facility, his heart is at home in those mountains. It never left. He is pictured below.

## Man Of The Mountains

We flow through the Rockies, my shadow and me,
like the pure, crystal streams, unbridled and free.
In the towns down below, I feel lonely and lost.
Though God might reside there, our paths seldom crossed.

But up in these mountains, clear up in the sky—
though there's nary another mortal nearby,
I feel close to a wonder that's grand as can be,
that beckons and welcomes the sad likes a' me.

Down below in the towns they're worshiping God,
but up in these mountains, I trek where he's trod.
I can hear his heart pulsing. I know that he's near;
and I feel a kinship with angels up here.

My shadow and me, we're both mountain men
who prefer to live in those mountains again.
My shadow and me prefer loftier air.
We're both mountain men and our hearts, they are there!

In the mountains with antelope, bighorn and deer—
In the mountains where grizzlies and cougars are near—
In the mountains, where eagles and falcons still glide—
that's where our hearts will forever reside.

# THE END OF AN ERA

Central to the myth and reality of the West is the American cowboy. His real life was a hard one and revolved around two annual roundups (spring and fall), the subsequent drives to market, and the time in the cattle towns spending his hard-earned money on food, clothing, gambling, and prostitution. On long drives, there was usually only one cowboy for each 250 head of cattle; and it was hard, grueling work. Cattle drives meant headaches, blisters, boils, and a cloud of flies.

It wasn't so much a "cattle drive" as a "cattle walk". The objective was to deliver the cattle as soon as possible in as good a physical condition as possible. So a herd might step off only twelve to fifteen miles a day. If a cowboy survived the two to three months of sudden hailstorms, lightning strikes, stampedes, thirst, and the clouds of dust, he could collect about $100 in wages. This was not much of a sum even in those days. During winter, when work on the range petered out, many cowboys hired on with ranches near the cattle towns, where they repaired and maintained buildings and equipment.

Six months after the Homestead Act of 1862 was passed, the Railroad Act was signed. By 1869, a transcontinental railroad extended across the frontier; and it became unnecessary to drive cattle long distances to market. The era of the great cattle drives had ended. Today, trucks as well as railroads transport cattle, so cattle drives are truly a relic of the past. In all, cattle drives boomed for only about thirty years, from the end of the Civil War to the late 1880s.

At the same time, the railroads spurred the westward movement of the homesteaders. The new railroads provided easy transportation for homesteaders and new immigrants who were lured westward by the railroad companies that were eager to sell off excess land at inflated prices. The new railroads provided ready access to needed goods; and catalog houses like Montgomery Ward offered weapons, barbed wire, farm tools, windows and doors, and other manufactured goods needed on the frontier.

Only about 40 percent of the homestead applicants completed the homestead requirements or obtained title to their homesteads. But in spite of this fact, approximately 1.6 million homesteads were granted and about 270 million acres (420,000 square miles) of federal land was obtained by homesteaders between 1862 and 1934. This amounts to a total of 10 percent of all lands in the United States. The Federal Land Use and Management Act of 1976 put an end to the homesteading era. The government believed the best use of the remaining public lands was for them to remain in government control. (The only exception was Alaska, for which the law allowed homesteading until 1986.)

# Cattle Drivin' Cowboy

I'm a cattle drivin' cowboy
who rides 18 wheeler rigs.
My job 's a haulin' cattle—
and it sure beats haulin' pigs.
My rig's revved up and roarin'.
It's all gassed up and greased.
With a load a' bawlin' cattle,
I'm headin' for the East.

Sometimes jus' t' pass the time
I think about the past;
and wish them days were back again-
and this time, that they'd last.
Sometimes when I'm on the road,
it gets t' feelin' real—
my hands are back a' holdin' reins
and not some steerin' wheel.

I'm back upon a saddle
and not this driver's seat.
I'm flyin' not on 18 wheels
but on some horses feet.
I've got an air conditioned rig
and soft upholstered seat;
and outside it's a' blisterin' hell
and folks 'r wiltin' in the heat.

I've got a bed inside the cab.
It's comfortable, of course;
but still I 'd chuck the lot a' it
t' be back on a horse.
I'm a cattle drivin' trucker;
but I wish that I could be
back on the range a herdin' steers
with a good horse under me.

# The Rancher's New Computer

After riding 'cross the plains
through tumbleweeds and sage,
he came back home and rode into
the new computer age.
He entered his computer
and the rancher felt the same
as Lewis & Clark most likely felt
when westward bound, they came.

The rancher, like the two of them,
rode through the vast unknown
to find a strange and hostile range
beyond his comfort zone.
Alone . . . uncertain . . . hesitant . . .
he fought his own "Star Wars"
while in the room across from him
his wife was doing chores.

While he was tearing out his hair,
she calmly fixed the bed.
He turned his new computer off,
and this is what he said:
"It's like a science fiction book
the things this box can do;
but it's a gonna blow m' fuse
before the month is through.

It helps me figure taxes out.
It finds the price a' beef.
The ranchin' chores this box can do—
are near beyond belief.
There's just one problem that I got—
learnin' how t' use it!
My temper gets the best a' me
each time that I peruse it!

I ain't a bad, hot tempered man.
I seldom lose my cool;
but this here box is turnin' me
into some screechin' fool!
"Stick with it Gramps", my grand kid said.
"It'll come, you'll see."
But what'll come, he didn't say.
I'd guess . . . insanity!

This new time wranglin's gonna craze
this old time head a' mine.
My old time heart keep tellin' me
the old time ways worked fine.
I'm just an old-time wrangler
on this new-time wranglin' range
And I sometime gets t' thinkin'
I'm too damn old t' change.

But this box ain't gonna beat me.
It's a matter now of pride.
There ain't a bronc that I can't break
or hoss that I can't ride.
I've beaten droughts and blizzards
and there's no way that ol' box
will outsmart, outdo, outshine
or outwit this ol' fox.

**Yee Haw!!!**

# The Times, They Are A Changin'

There are hundreds of breeds of cattle in the world. During the era of the open range, the Texas Longhorns were the prized breed. This was due to their hardiness and ability to endure in harsh terrain. Then came the decades long era of the Hereford. Most folks would agree that Hereford cattle led the way in revolutionizing beef production in America. This was largely due to their ability to get fat at an early age and to produce the ideal in "baby beef". But slowly there was a change taking place in the meat-packing industry and in the basic American consumer's diet. The result was that beef packers paid less for fat cattle. A different variety of stock was preferred; a trimmer, leaner kind with less fat and more red meat. Black Angus cattle fit that description. The leaner quality of Angus beef is the focus of numerous current advertising promotions, including Certified Angus Beef in supermarkets and the use and promotion of 100 percent Angus beef by many restaurants.

### *Yesterday's Breed*

There's a farmer who raises blue ribbon beef
whose barnyard is just down the road.
It used to be crammed with Black Angus steers,
but he recently shipped out load.
Well, I took me a walk and I had me a talk
with the stock that remained yesterday.
The barnyard was bare. Just two Herefords were there;
and I swear I heard one of them say:

*That Black Angus crowd was plumb snooty and proud.*
*They looked down on Matilda and me.*
*They leered and they jeered and so caustically sneered-*
*'cuz we wuz just Herefords, y' see.*
*We were yesterday's breed, the Black Angus agreed;*
*and we didn't dispute their belief.*
*Even Ronald at Big Mac's McDonald, no less,*
*was wantin' just Black Angus beef.*

*Now Hardee's and Harvey's and fine uptown grills
serve their customers certified meat;
and Matilda 'n me think that's just fine. You see
it's them Black Angus dudes that they eat.
When we woke up at dawn, we wuz here! They wuz gone!
We wuz happy as Herefords can get.
We wuz filled with such cheer becuz we wuz still here.
and it ain't us that's gonna get "ett"!*

# The Water Wars

Nearly 131 years ago, the Lakota and Cheyenne Indians battled the 7th U.S. Cavalry in the Battle Of The Little Big Horn. In this same area, a new battle is taking place. The water dispute between Wyoming and Montana regarding flows in the Powder and Tongue Rivers is so contentious, one Montana official said it is almost enough to start a war. Water meant survival in the West. Many of the range wars fought in the Old West, concerned water and water rights. It remains a source of much litigation today.

On January 8th, 2011, the U.S. Supreme Court appointed a special master to investigate allegations by Montana that Wyoming is withholding more water than it is entitled to. This latest intervention follows a line of bickering and disagreement between the neighboring states over water rights that have centered on the Tongue and Powder rivers. According to Montana their share of the water is being depleted by Wyoming's excessive water use.

The Tongue and Powder rivers flow through northern Wyoming and southern Montana before draining into the Yellowstone River. The 1950 Yellowstone River Compact, which allocates each state a share of the water and its tributaries, is being violated by the water usage practices of Wyoming according to Montana. Montana further states that the leaching of river water is harming its consumers and farmers who rely on it. (While North Dakota is a party to the 1950 Compact, it is not active in this suit.)

Under traditional water law that applies in the arid and semi-arid Western states, the first person who makes use of water for a "beneficial" use has the priority right to continue using it for that purpose, but loses it if the use is discontinued. The "beneficial" use at issue in this lawsuit is for irrigation. Under this concept, as a river flows downstream, those users situated on the higher reaches with rights can withdraw water and, if not limited in quantities, can deplete the flow so that less water flows downstream to users in the lower reaches. With the Yellowstone rising initially in Wyoming, its water users are in a position to influence how much water goes downstream into Montana.

In 2004 and 2006, Montana attempted to negotiate with Wyoming to increase the water flows downstream. In 2007, however, when these negotiations proved unsuccessful, Montana sued Wyoming, arguing that Wyoming is using water that should be delivered downstream, and that it is also pumping underground water reserves to irrigate farmland that should feed into the two rivers. Underground water supplies are also pumped extensively as part of the process of coal bed methane production.

In addition, Montana has drawn up new water quality standards that affect the Tongue and Powder rivers, contending that three years ago, something happened to the water, causing the once-rich soil in Custer County, Montana to turn into mud with the consistency of mayonnaise. The soils could not hold the plant material, and within weeks, large sections of crops turned yellow and died. They believe that the culprit was salt in the river water, which when mixed with clay soils turned the cropland into a soggy mush. (Montana state regulators believe the high salt content is at least partly the result of deep groundwater extraction by coal-bed methane (CBM) operations in neighboring Wyoming — one of the nation's leading producers of coal-bed methane. The water, pumped by the millions of gallons from coal seams to help coax gas to the surface, is then routinely pumped back into the Tongue River and other watersheds by CBM operators, where it indiscriminately mixes with downstream water supplies.)

This is not the only dispute over water issues between the two states. Each of the states has been trying to gain a greater share of the Bighorn River, another tributary of the Yellowstone to the West. Back when the Bighorn River flowed strongly out of the Wind River mountains, it backed up to a man-made lake that once drew almost half a million visitors annually. Bighorn Lake extends for 71 miles through Montana and Wyoming (31 of the miles are in Wyoming). But for eight years drought has choked the river, chopping 30 miles off the Bighorn Lake near Lovell, Wyoming. This has caused tourists to go elsewhere. And now Wyoming argues that Montana is just trying to tap the reservoir to feed a downstream trout fishery that could end Lovell's recreational plans for good.

As demand for water increases and water in the arid Western states becomes even scarcer, more of these disputes are likely to crop up. As the worst dry spell since the 1930s shows no signs of abating, many states are squabbling with each other and federal officials. Nebraska and Kansas are wrangling for control of irrigation water from the Republican River. South Dakota has demanded the Army Corps of Engineers stop drawing down reservoirs in the state because it is hurting recreational fishing. Barge companies along the Missouri River in Iowa are demanding the Corps release more water so their vessels can operate.

In the Old West there were bitter feuds, often between rifle-brandishing cowboys, over who had the right to the precious water that always seemed to be in short supply on the sun-baked prairie. Today, in this modern era, these "water wars" continue, but now the combatants are states, and the weapon of choice is the legal brief.

*Fight For The Waterhole* by Frederick Remington (1901)

### Muddy Water

In the arid arroyo they found it.
Water! They clustered around it.
Water! Not much of it . . . .
barely a touch of it.
Muddy! Who cared! It was water!

In the heat, furnace-hot,
they fought off the drought.
Their tongues turned to kiln-fired clay.
It hurt when they cursed
their God-awful thirst
and the winds that were blasting away.
The streams all around were bone dry;

and the springs that they'd found . . . . alkali.
Their thirst . . . unsurpassed!
Sweet water at last!
Muddy! Who cared! It was water!

They'd earlier found
in the cracked, withered ground
a pool the hue of black ink.
The water was rank;
and the pool itself stank—
and yet they were tempted to drink.
Sweet water! They cupped it with haste.
Sweet water!
They'd die for a taste.
There's none there would doubt it . . .
they'd perish without it.
Muddy! Who cared! It was water!

They'd fight for it. Maybe they'd die.
It was theirs.
Just let somebody try
to pry it away . . . .
it's a high price they'd pay!
Muddy! Who cared! It was WATER!

# The Chronic Farm/Ranch Crisis

The following comments are excerpts taken from *The Missoula Independent*, October 7, 1999:

"Regardless of the size of the farm or the commodity being raised, all farming and ranching operates according to a very simple mathematical formula: How much does it cost to raise a product, and how much is the farmer paid to bring that product to market? Eventually, a farmer falls below the break-even point, where the cost of production is higher than what the product is sold for, and it becomes cheaper not to farm, or to simply sell off the land. Increasingly, that is the scenario unfolding on scores of Montana's family farms. When you don't have enough collateral to cover your debt, you know you're in trouble."

"The price we pay at the checkout stand bears little relationship to the cost to the farmer or rancher to raise that product. When the farmer takes his product to market, be it the local grain elevator, the nearest feed lot or the slaughterhouse, in most cases he has but two choices: either sell that product at the asking price of the corporation that operates as a virtual monopoly, or hold onto it and hope that the price is higher when he returns next week. . . ."

"Occasionally, a farmer can exercise a third option and drive his produce or livestock 100, 200 or even 500 miles down the road and try to get a better price at the next grain elevator or feed lot. But more times than not, that market is run by the same corporation that operates in his hometown, and whatever slight profit he might see is more than offset by the cost of transporting the goods in the first place . . . ."

"Which leads to yet another monopoly that Montana producers face: only one railroad that serves the entire state. As a result, according to the Alliance for Railway Competition, Montana growers pay among the highest rail rates in the nation. Grain producers in Nebraska can ship their grain to Portland for less than it costs Montana farmers. The reason: Nebraska is served by two railroads."

Montana farmer, Bob Christ of the Christ Ranch near Skalkaho Creek just south of Hamilton, Montana said, "I have three sons. They'd love to ranch. But there's just no money in it."

As one farmer joked bitterly:

> *Agriculture has become a form of child abuse: You bequeath your troubles to your children. Little wonder, then, that the number one cause of death among farmers and ranchers last year was suicide. Sociologists speculate that at least half of the deaths caused by machinery each years are intentional, by farmers who want to ensure that their families collect their life insurance.*

# Cattle Country Trilogy

The following three poems were written during the height of the 1980's recession. At that time I was Director of the Regulatory Division, and legal counsel for the Iowa Department of Agriculture. I served in that capacity for 10 years; and during that time, I met with farmers across the State of Iowa. The 1980's Recession was a farm crisis . . . but more significantly, it was a severe human crisis.

In Hills, Iowa, a farmer killed his banker, his neighbor, his wife, and then himself. Near Ruthton, Minnesota, a farmer and his son murdered two bank officials. In South Dakota's Union County, a Farmers Home Administration (FmHA) administrator killed his wife, daughter, son, and dog before committing suicide. In the note he left behind he claimed the pressures of his job became too much for him to bear.

The economy that led to thousands of bankruptcies and foreclosures in the Great Depression of the 30s played out to a lesser degree in the recession of the 80s. It continues today; and the number of family farms and ranches continues to decline. As George Santayanna wrote:

*Those who cannot remember the past, are condemned to repeat it.*

### The Sweat Belongs To Me

The banker owns this ranch of mine . . .
but all the misery,
and pain and sweat that goes with it-
well, that belongs t' me.
While I might hold the title,
until it's free and clear-
the banker owns my ranch, my barns,
each heifer, bull and steer.

He lets me know who owns it
when I'm late repaying loans.
While I might own the title,
the rest the banker owns.
Y' take a loan out on your place
when profit's t' be had-
but sooner, more than later,
the economy turns bad.

Recessions and Depressions
always hit the farmers first;
and farmers are the first t' pay
when the bubbles burst.
My grandpa used t' tell me,
"Avoid the mortgage trap . . .
Y' go t' bed with bankers,
y' end up with the clap."

But I believed the Big Boys.
I thought that they were wise.
"Expand . . . buy new equipment . . .
y 'gotta modernize . . ."
And now the banker owns my ranch
and my machinery.
While I might hold the title,
the sweat belong t' me.

## Mad Dog Mean

Mad dog mean, the times are . . . .
and it just turned snarlin' rough.
It happened just awhile ago.
They carted off my stuff.
This ranch has been my families
for near a hundred years.
The bank's a gonna auction it.
Too bad they can't sell tears.
If only they could sell my tears,
there'd be enough t' pay
back taxes and delinquent loans
and wipe this grief away.

They loaded Grandma's poster bed,
her chiffonier and such.
The chances are that none a' it
will bring too awful much.
The times are mean and ugly . . . .
this day's a snarlin' bitch.

If only I was someone else.
If only I was rich.
The fact is, I ain't none a' that.
I'm just a rancher's wife
who's never known or wanted
another way of life.

If only I could melt away
and join the auction crowd,
and bid on Grandma's poster bed,
and walk with head unbowed.
Great Grandma gave the bed t' her
when she was just a bride.
I watched my Grandma make the bed;
then polish it with pride.
I've known a lot of hard times-
but this sure beats all I've seen.
The times have sunk their teeth in me.
It just turned mad dog mean.

## Tom and Me

**A**ll I ever wanted was
t' ranch on Grandpa's place.
It's hard for me acceptin'
that with Tom, that ain't the case.
Tom, he'll be th' last one
t' bear our family name.
I never could quite understand . . . .
he didn't feel the same.

With me and those before me,
we were fixtures on this land.
With Tom, the ranch means nothin'
but some greenbacks in our hand.
Tom, he wanted somethin' else . . . .
a different life and place.
And Tom was filled with memories
that time did not erase.

He watched while Banion lost his ranch
and everything he owned.
It didn't bring enough t' pay
the funds th' bank had loaned.
And one day Banion shot himself....
and we were filled with grief.
But Tom was filled with bitterness
and rage beyond belief

Then Tom went off t' college;
and became an engineer.
He found a decent payin' job
a thousand miles from here.
We always made a livin'-
though I can't say that we thrived.
But still, when others bellied up,
Tom and me survived.

But Tom would often urge me
t' blaze some brand new trail;
and come the next inflation,
t' list the ranch for sale.
I used t' think I'd never sell.
My sweat's in every clod;
in every furrow on this land,
my life's plowed in the sod.

Now lately, I have wondered;
maybe Tom is right.
This gettin' old is somethin'
that is mighty hard t' fight.
My back and joints are tellin' me
that this time I can't win.
There comes a time for givin up-
a time for givin' in.

And thus it is ... There goes another family farm!
*Time after time they're taken on an economic sleigh ride;*
*And one by one, their struggling kind, are falling by the way side.*
*Bette Wolf Duncan*

# TOMBSTONES ON THE PRAIRIE

*"The Little House That Grew"* © 2006, Jeri Dobrowski,
Lamesteer Publishing; 1471 Carlyle Road S; Beach, ND 58621-9650

    This is a photo of a homestead house that grew with the needs and prosperity of a pioneering family. It stands alongside North Dakota State Highway #16 in the western part of the state, in Golden Valley County, North Dakota. It was photographed late in the day in July, 2006. Jeri Dobrowski says that the past several years have not been kind to the assemblage of wood and mortar; and that it is beginning to falter at an alarming rate. She is fearful the next time she passes by she'll find that it has been burned or dozed. She says that a barn that was in the same yard has been razed. She feels that it's a matter of time before the photo is all that remains of one family's time spent on the Plains. As it is, she is taken by its beauty every time she see it.

    It's such a beautiful photograph, but it fills me with sadness every time I see it. It reminds me . . . It reminds me of the ranch house I was born in . . . It reminds me of an era that is no more . . . Just tombstones on the prairie.

# The Broken Hearted House

Abandoned, sad, old derelict;
it waits upon the plains,
scoffing at the storms that lash
its weathered, worn remains.
Waiting, waiting, waiting
for a family long time gone.
The house just stands there waiting
but the folks have all moved on.

The parents both are long since dead.
Two sons died in the War.
The other kids are married
and don't live there anymore.
As winds whip through its crumbling cracks,
a scampering, camping mouse
listens to the moaning
of the broken hearted house.

A nearby weeping willow
sheds floods of leafy tears
as the broken hearted derelict
remembers bygone years;
recalls its humble start-up
when the family was quite small,
and three rooms and an attic loft
sufficed to house them all.

But then the little family
into a large one, grew;
and like the ever swelling flock,
the little house did too.
A wing grew on the east side;
and another on the west.
The family grew and prospered,
and the house was richly blessed.

It remembers still the baking bread
that always smelled so great;
and the family round the table
saying grace before they ate;
and the rooms that rang with laughter
and, most times, with good cheer.
And everything about it said,
"A family's living here!"

Now the sad old house stands waiting,
just waiting there bereft;
waiting for the happy clan
that long ago all left.
The winds race down the chimney
and go rumbling down the halls,
and flog a whip of prairie grit
upon the crumbling walls.

When the storms rip through the windows,
you can hear the sad house groan;
and in the battered attic,
you can hear the timbers drone.
Outside an owl and, now and then,
a sharp-tailed prairie grouse
hoot in cruel derision
at the broken hearted house.

# BIBLIOGRAPHY

## LOUISIANA PURCHASE

Sprague, Marshall. *So Vast So Beautiful a Land: Louisiana and the Purchase.* (1974), Little, Brown and Company,1974.

- Hosmer, J.K., *The History of the Louisiana Purchase,* (1902)

  Malone, Michael P. et al; *Montana—A History of Two Centuries;* (1991); Seattle: University of Washington Press. p. 30.

  Fleming, Thomas; *The Louisiana Purchase*; (1972); John Wiley & Sons, Inc., P:149

**Lewis and Clark Expedition:**

Robert Miller. *Native America, Discovered and Conquered: Thomas Jefferson, Lewis and Clark, and Manifest Destiny*
    Bison Books, 2008.

David Lavender. *The Way to the Western Sea*, University of Nebraska Press, 2001.

James Ronda. *Lewis and Clark among the Indians*, University of Nebraska Press, 2002.

**Sacrifice Cliff:**

Simms, T. J., *Traditions of the Crows*, (1903).

Yellowstone Genealogy Forum, *"Sacrifice Cliff & Skeleton Cliff"*; Summary Details-Continuing Investigation; March 15, 2006 (Records kept at Parmly Billings Library, 510 North 2th Street; Billings, MT 59101)

*"Pioneers of Eastern Montana—The Legend of Sacrifice Cliff"*; The Billings Gazette, May 29, 1971;

**Red River Rose:**

*"The Red River Carts"*, History & Culture, Minnesota Territorial Pioneers. Citing to the newspaper, Minnesota Democrat, St. Paul, MN, July 22, 1851.

Blegen, Theodore C & Jordan, Philip D, *"With Various Voices: Recordings Of North Star Life"*, 291-294; The Itasca Press; St. Paul, MN (1949).

*"Red River Carts"*, Regional Studies at North Dakota State University; Fargo, ND.

Gilman, Rhoda R. et al, *"The Red River Trails: Oxcart Routes Between St. Paul and the Selkirk Settlement, 1820—1870"*, p.5, Minnesota Historical Society Press, St. Paul, MN.

**DAKOTA TERRITORY**

Smith, Colonel to Gen. Ord, June 27, 1873, Department of the Platte, Letters Received, National Archives. (Colonel Smith was commander of the 14th Infantry, headquartered at Fort Laramie, who had extensive experience with the Lakota.)

Liberty, Dr. Margo, *"Cheyenne Primacy: The Tribes Perspective As Opposed To That Of The United States Army; A Possible Alternative To The Great Sioux War Of 1876"*, Friends of The Little Bighorn; http://www.friendslittlebigorn.com/cheyenneprimacy.htm

Hyde, George, *"Red Cloud's Folk: A History of the Ogalala Sioux Indians"*, University of Oklahoma Press, 1937)

Schell Herbert S., *History of South Dakota*, Lincoln, University of Nebraska Press, 1975.

Forbis, William H. et al, *The Cowboys* (New York: Time-Life books, 1973; *Hunting Trips of a Ranchman,* Atlantic Monthly, July—December 1885, 563—565.

Dantz, William T., *Theodore Roosevelt—Cowboy and Ranchman: A Cowboy's Reminiscences of the President's Cowboy Experiences as a Ranchman in the Bad Lands Of North Dakota,* Harpers Weekly, August 6, 1904.

Packard, A. T., *Roosevelt's Ranching Days: The Outdoor Training of a President as a Man among Men*, Saturday Evening Post, March 4, 1905, 13-14.

New York Times, *Paying Cattle Ranches: A Thriving Industry in the Northwest* and *Dressed Beef in the West: The Business Enterprise of the Marquis de Mores*; September 21, 1884 and February 25, 1884.

**Red River Valley Early Pioneers:**

Libby, O.G., *Collections of the State Historical Society of North Dakota*, Vol. IV.(1913).

Lounsberry, Colonel Clement A, *Early History of North Dakota*, (1919).

## MONTANA TERRITORY

Fazio, John C.;, *"How The Civil War Was Won In Virginia City, Montana"*; The Montana Pioneer, November 2010, see page 24 et seq Fazio, John C., *"The Vigilantes of Montana"*, The Cleveland Civil War Roundtable; http://clevelandcivilwarroundtable.com/articles/society/montana_vigilantes.htm Lewis, David S.; *"Montana's Ties To The Confederate South"*, Montana Pioneer; http://www.mtpioneer.com/2010-Nov-confederate.html

Albright, R. E., *"The American Civil War Was A Factor In Montana Territorial Politics"*, Pacific Historical Review, Vol.6, No. 1 (Mar., 1937), University of California Press.

National Park Service, U.S. Department of Interior, *Garvin Basin and Cattle Rustling,* http://www.nps.gov/bica/historyculture/garvin-basin-and-cattle-rustling.htm

## STATE OF MONTANA

"*The Homestead Act of 1862*"; The National Archives; http://www.archives.gov/education/lessons/homestead-act/

"*Homestead Act: Who Were The Settlers? The Civil War Connection*"; Nebraska Studies; http://www.nebraskastudies.org/0500/stories/0501_0202.html

Sargent, Tom; "*The Commanding Officers in Montana & The Economics of the Civil War, The Civil War in Montana*";Virginia City Preservation Alliance, 1999.

## Mountain Man

Metz, Jered; "*The Last Eleven Days Of Earl Durand*"; High Plains Press, 2005 ISBN 0-**931271-7**2-X

## Depression/Recession Years in Montana

Nebraska Studies.org; *Crisis in Agriculture*
*http://www.nebraskastudies.org/1000/frameset_reset.html*
*http://www.nebraskastudies.org/1000/stories/1001_0100.html*

Browning, Skylar (Editor);*Missoula Independent;* October 7, 1999; *http://missoulanews.bigskypress.com/missoula/will-farm-for-food/ Content?oid=1132182*

McRae, W.C. et al; *Moon Montana; The Dust Bowl Years;* pages 439, et.seq.: Avalon Publishing;7th Edition (2009).

Malone, Michael P et al; *Montana: A History of Two Centuries, Drought, Depression, and War;* pages 281 et seq.; University of Washington Press (1976), Revised edition, 6th printing (2003)

## End of an Era

"*It's your misfortune and none of my own";* A new history of the American West; University of Oklahoma Press, ISBN 0-8061-2366-4

Zeidel, Robert F. ; *"Peopling the Empire: The Great Northern Railroad and the Recruitment of Immigrant Settlers to North Dakota,"* North Dakota History, 1993, Vol. 60 Issue 2, 14-23.

**The Water Wars**

Wiel, Samuel C.; *Water Rights in the Western States* (3rd ed.1911).

*Yellowstone River Compact; Pub.L.No. 82-231, 65 Stat. 663 (1951).*

*State of Montana vs. States of Wyoming and North Dakota;* In the Supreme Court of the United States; Case No. 137, 2010;

Edwards Brothers,Inc!
Thorofare, NJ 08086
22 March, 2011
BA2011081